Mothers in Israel

Deslee Campbell

Published by Deslee Campbell, 2024.

While every precaution has been taken in the preparation of this book, the publisher assumes no responsibility for errors or omissions, or for damages resulting from the use of the information contained herein.

MOTHERS IN ISRAEL

First edition. May 27, 2024.

Copyright © 2024 Deslee Campbell.

ISBN: 979-8215257098

Written by Deslee Campbell.

Table of Contents

MOTHERS IN ISRAEL

Prologue

Increasingly in these days of rapid social and economic change women find themselves tossed too and fro by many new waves. Every social change brings greater demands, major role and identity changes, new freedoms, and, ironically enough, new restrictions. For example, the self-concept of the woman during the hey-day of the feminist revolution is not the same as her self-concept during the backlash against feminism. The revolution that appeared to promise much has left women to make their way in a different world and with greater and more diverse burdens to carry than at any time since poor women were the char ladies of the East End in Victorian London.

While women can be very easily 'lost at sea' in these tidal waves of change, there is a firm anchorage, a moral absolute amidst all the uncertainty. In secular parlance this is called the Judeo/Christian ethic. It includes the eternal principles and the teachings, practical applications, and behaviours, laid down first in the Jewish Scripture, expounded upon in the New Testament. These are the moral certainties of the centuries, everything else is fashion, mere decoration, new trends or perhaps simply ethically wrong.

While the vast bulk of Scriptural material is applicable to both men and women, most of the narrative content centres on the main male personalities, the

chief Biblical heroes. Interestingly, these characters
are 'painted warts and all' and we can be forgiven for
thinking how similar to us they really were, as we
know all about their weaknesses, as well as their
strengths.

We could also be forgiven for thinking that the Biblical
heroines were all virtue. The narrative majors on the
wonderful deeds they did and the important
contributions they made. Rarely are they developed
'in the round'. The dark side of their characters, their
times of failure and weakness, are ignored. Perhaps
they were always strong and noble and courageous.
Certainly they would have had to have been out standing
exemplars of virtuous and victorious
womanhood.

There are some vital Biblical passages of direct
teaching for and about women, such as the eulogy of
the Virtuous Wife, from the last chapter of Proverbs,
but by and large it is the example set by the Biblical
heroines, both married and single, which provides
women with role models; anchors in these troubled
times. There are obviously many almost concealed
spiritual truths and lessons in the lives of the women
of Israel.

Principles of godly woman-hood can be deduced,
following a study of those regarded as worthy of
emulation. Interestingly, such study neither reveals a
picture of feminine learned or feigned helplessness,
languid inaction, or repressed 'church-mousiness';
nor one of pseudo-masculinity. The Biblical heroine

MOTHERS IN ISRAEL

was all woman, but she was quite a gal!!!

Chapter 1

Who is Our Mother?
Many years ago I was challenged by this question: If
God is our father, whom does the Bible teach is our
mother? I have long pondered the question of
'spiritual motherhood'. By learning about our spiritual
mother we can begin to understand what it means to be 'a
mother in Israel'.

Plate 1.1. 'Ha Tikvah' (The Hope).
Sculpture by Nicky Imber in Safed to symbolise
Israel's birth.

DESLEE CAMPBELL

Since the Shoah children have been Israel's hope
for the future.
Photo: D. Campbell, 1994.

MOTHERS IN ISRAEL

Some of the mainline denominations teach of 'Holy Mother Church', but there is only minimal evidence that Scripture teaches that this is the answer; although from two excerpts from II John, which refer to "the chosen lady and her children", it could, perhaps, be deduced that the church is our mother. St Paul, however, makes a clear statement that answers the question. He clearly states that the New Jerusalem, the heavenly city, the Jerusalem-From-Above is our mother: "The Jerusalem that is above is free, and she is our mother." (Gal. 4:26) In Hebrew the name of each town or city (singular) is, grammatically speaking, feminine. It is as though, in the distant past, each town was considered a mother to its citizens, just as, today, every ship we sail in is called 'she'. Certainly, from a Biblical standpoint, a city or town, which provides shelter and protection, can be referred to as 'a mother in Israel', as in II Samuel where a wise woman said to Joab: "We are the peaceful and faithful in Israel. You are trying to destroy a city that is a mother in Israel."(II Sam.20:19)

The idea of a city as our mother is therefore quite consistent with Jewish religious thought. Consequently St Paul is free to idealise the Heavenly Jerusalem as our mother, as he does in the fourth chapter of his letter to the Galatians. It is a metaphor. We may at once contrast this idea with another Biblical metaphor, this one from the Book of Revelation. Here this city, New Jerusalem, is likened

to a bride, beautifully adorned. It reads:
"I saw the Holy City, the new Jerusalem,
coming down out of heaven from God,
prepared as a bride beautifully dressed for her
husband." (Rev. 21:2)

Here is a mystery. Is the New Jerusalem a bride, or a mother? The writer of Revelation wrote that the Holy City is presented from the Heavenlies as a bride, she is like a bride. Can she also be a mother? Perhaps she may be both at the same time - a mother who is as beautiful within, and still as well-presented outwardly, as on the day of her wedding. Perhaps Galatians and Revelations may not present contradictory imagery after all.

Turning in detail to what Paul wrote about the cities he calls earthly and heavenly Jerusalem, we find another seeming contradiction, one between Isaiah and Paul. Isaiah spoke of earthly Jerusalem as a beloved city and a mother, at least the mother of the Jewish people, if not the mother of us all, when he exhorted:

> *"Rejoice with Jerusalem and be glad for her, all
> you who love her; rejoice greatly all you who
> mourn over her. For you will nurse and be
> satisfied at her comforting breasts; you will
> drink deeply and delight in her overflowing
> abundance...... you will nurse and be carried on
> her arm and dandled on her knees." (Is. 66:10-*
12)

While Paul regards earthly Jerusalem as one who has

children, his attitude does, at first reading, appear to contradict Isaiah's idea of this city when Paul wrote: "These things may be taken figuratively, for the women (Sarah and Hagar) represent two covenants. One covenant is from Mt. Sinai and bears children who are to be slaves: This is Hagar. Now Hagar stands for Mt. Sinai in Arabia and corresponds to the present city of Jerusalem, because she is in slavery with her children. But the Jerusalem that is above is free, and she is our mother." (Gal. 4:24-27)

This is a dilemma: is the earthly city a mother, as Isaiah says? Is she our mother? Or is she a slave-woman, a city not considered worthy of our respect, love or praise?

Alternatively the two cities of Jerusalem mentioned by Paul, earthly and heavenly Jerusalem, may be, as Paul suggests in Galatians 4:24, purely allegories. They may be representative of groups of people, rather than physical locations, that is, people with certain spiritual qualities. Perhaps, figuratively speaking, these metaphors refer to people bound in legalism, versus those characterised by freedom in the Spirit. Whatever the interpretation, Paul clearly stated that he was indeed writing figuratively.

In addressing this issue, what is significant is that the New Jerusalem, while given From Above, is not an entirely new spiritual identity, but the spiritual heir of her forebear. She will bear the same name as her predecessor, the original Jerusalem, and will stand in the same location (though she will cover a huge area, compared with present day Jerusalem).

Scripture indicates many similarities between the destinies of the new and the ancient city. Consider the similarity in architecture, decoration, and citizenry outlined by the following passage. The new Jerusalem will have foundations of precious stones and each of her gates will be made of one pearl. It is said of her: "The wall was made of jasper, and the city of pure gold, as pure as glass. The foundations of the city walls were decorated with every kind of precious stone. The first foundation was jasper, the second sapphire, the third chalcedony, the fourth emerald, the fifth sardonyx, the sixth carnelian, the seventh chrysolite, the eighth beryl ... each gate was made of a single pearl. The street of the city was of pure gold, like transparent glass." (Rev. 21:18-19)

"Nothing impure will ever enter it, nor will anyone who does what is shameful or deceitful, but only those whose names are written in the Lamb's book of life" (v. 27).

Now compare this with what Isaiah foretold about the future which the Lord plans for that oft' afflicted city, earthly Jerusalem, that is, plans concerning her architecture and her citizens:

> *"O afflicted city, lashed by storms and not comforted, I will build you with stones of turquoise, your foundations with sapphires. I*

will make your battlements of rubies, your
gates of sparkling jewels, and all your walls of
precious stones. All your sons will be taught by
the Lord and great will be your children's
peace. In righteousness you will be
established: Tyranny will be far from you; and
you will have nothing to fear." (Is. 54:11-14)

Both Isaiah and John of Revelations speak of a city of peace, righteousness, beauty and tranquillity. There is obviously a spiritual, as well as a geographic and architectural continuum between the two, that is, between the earthly and heavenly Jerusalems. Paul and Isaiah both refer to the same city.

Returning to the fourth chapter of the Epistle to the Galatians we find that the problematic passage appears to disparage the earthly Jerusalem, which Paul corresponds with Mt. Sinai, with its legal restrictions, in contrast to heavenly Jerusalem, with its purity and freedom in the Spirit.

The truth, however, is not so simple. This passage must be carefully read and analysed. Clearly, as Paul would have known perfectly well, the Jewish people are not, historically, the children of Hagar. Hagar was Ishmael's mother, and the Arab people claim descent from her. The Jewish people certainly do not!! They claim descent from Sarah, and her son Isaac, who was the 'son of promise'. Therefore Paul's words about the city are not intended to be read literally; and they must not be read literally.

Paul clearly states that the two women, Hagar and

Sarah, are simply used in a limited, symbolic sense, that is, 'figuratively'. The metaphorical meaning is, Paul admits, hidden here. That is what is important. Hagar was a servant woman, bound by Sarah's will, to be given to Abraham, or to be expelled from his presence at her mistresses' command. In her legal servitude Hagar represents those under Law, even under Sinai's Law, as implemented in Jerusalem in that period.

This passage, (Galatians 4:21-31) does not denote a simplistic dichotomy between "Hagar = legalism = Jews" on the one hand, and "Sarah = holiness and freedom in the Spirit = Christians" on the other. The real meaning is less obvious, more abstract and more figurative.

While Judaism could be legalistic and 'in bondage' so could Christianity. Paul urged the Galatian believers not to turn their faith into legalism. This can happen so easily, even today. Many Christian groups impose strict rules, such as rules about dress, food, cosmetics, hair-styles and head coverings; as well as things like giving, submission, baptismal formulae and permissible activities for Sundays. Christianity can so easily become: "Hagar = legalism = Christian". Conversely we know that many of the Old Testament notables lived in the freedom of Ruach Ha Kodesh (the Holy Spirit). Such people included David, the man after God's own heart; Samuel, who, even as a child, spoke with God and was dedicated as a Nazarite from birth; Moses, who saw His Glory; and a great many others. Of these Jewish heroes we should most certainly write: "Sarah = holiness and freedom-in-the-Spirit = Jewish."

Paul's actual meaning is: "Those who are led by the Spirit of God are sons of God" (i.e., sons of promise) (Rom. 8:14). We must therefore conclude that the city which is our mother, our nurturer and protector, is a spiritual entity, ruled by the Spirit of the Almighty, neither Jewish nor Christian, but holy, godly and beautiful: in fact she is as 'the Kingdom of God' in which we are meant to live.

Paul, while he grappled with the very primal interface of Jewish-Christian encounter, certainly did not denigrate the Jewish people, and continued, throughout his life, to regard himself as an observant Jew, proud of his heritage. Paul also esteemed the guidance of Ruach Ha Kodesh and that quality of personal relationship with God in which each of the prophets and saints of the Old Testament walked. Of course freedom in the Spirit does not mean licence, and it does not mean the over-throw of the Law, quite the opposite. The Torah, or Law, is not to be dispensed with but will one day be written on all of our hearts so that keeping it will be simple, not an imposition, and certainly not a form of slavery: "*I will put my law in their minds and write it on their hearts. I will be their God, and they will be my people.*" (Jer. 31:33)

Such people as these, with transformed hearts, are

those who are to be citizens of `the Kingdom of God' and `Jerusalem-From-Above'. All will be born of the Spirit of God. At present, however, everything on this earth, even Jerusalem, like every city, is subject to corruption, imperfection, and the judgements of the Law; and she is certainly not more sinful than any other city. Yet in the midst of the earthly, the imperfect, we can live in the Kingdom From on High. Eventually, at a time to come, the distinction between the corrupt and the perfect, the earthly and the heavenly, the human and the Divine, will be wiped away. By the Power of God, the legal and the spiritual will become one. Earthly Jerusalem, and her children will be caught up into the New. In that city there will be no evil: neither will there be the results of evil: mourning, pain, and tears. Therefore we will all dwell happily within her.

"There will be no more death
or mourning or crying or pain, for the old order
of things has passed away." (Rev. 21:4)

As the world around us grows darker we all look forward to that day, that Messianic kingdom, that paradise, or, as Israelis say, `Gan Eden'.

Chapter 2

Qualities of Motherhood.

1) . Many infants are born
red, wrinkled, misshapen, even deformed. "Only a
mother could love them" we say, and rightly so. Good
mothers give unconditional love. Mother-hearts do
not switch off their love when their child is soiled,
grubby, or naughty. Such love does not need to be
deserved, or earned.

2) . An emotional need
for her own love to be reciprocated makes a mother
desire to have a baby who snuggles, cuddles and
responds warmly, especially while breast feeding.
This delights the mothers' heart. It is a cruel blow to
have a stiff, rejecting infant, especially one who
refuses the breast altogether. Yet mothers are
continually willing to give, even when bonding love is
absent.

3) This is a physical longing.
The nursing mother has a physical need to feed her
infant. When baby over-sleeps at feeding time the
mother can be torn between her own need to feed
and her reluctance to awaken the baby. Where a
child's appetite is reduced, for example in illness,
there can even be a painful physical need for the
infant to be successfully suckled. Aspects of this
continue into later life - spurned love is very painful.

4) . There is no record of

the prodigal son's mother. If his father longed to see his face once again, how much more so his mother?

A mother loves her child no matter how much distance separates them. It is an enduring love, despite the conduct, or forgetfulness, of the child. It has been said that being a mother is to face a lifetime of having one's heart walking around outside of one's body. The 'prodigal-mother' experience is one of the most painful.

5) The wayward child, who,
like the 'prodigal son', has 'blown every opportunity' continues to be loved by his, or her, mother. It is mothers who, more than any others, put into practice the principle of being willing to forgive "seventy times seven."

6) Many new mothers
find that they view their baby as a 'little stranger', hardly knowing which end to hold onto, frightened 'it' will break! Motherhood grows on such women - it doesn't arrive, gift wrapped with flowers, at the hospital.

In every case though, the relationship
between mother and child is a process of growth and change, of learning in the College of Real Life Experiences, the place where the most enduring lessons are learnt.

7) The relationship
must change and develop as the child struggles towards independence and adulthood. As the old saying goes: the 'aprons strings' must be untied

(preferably a gradual process). This is rarely a smooth transition, and is often painful for both parties. Through all of these experiences the true mother's commitment will remain.

8) . If there is a supreme
principle governing this present age it is Self: self-gratification, self-enhancement, self-will. This is the direct anthesis of the merciful love of God, the sacrificial route to Calvary and the agonising Gethsemane challenge:

> *"Father, if you are willing, take this cup from*
> *me; yet not my will, but yours be done."* (Lk.
22:42)

`Calvary' and `Gethsemane' are unpopular concepts in today's church where big is better, first is best, and suffering is seen as sinful. But they are not my words.... I did not write them in the Bible nor demand that they become an authentic part of the experience of Faith.

Parenthood, and motherhood in particular, is the place where selfishness finally meets its match, where we must transcend self-centred immaturity; where we learn that we cannot have everything we want, just made to order. For some this is easy, for others it is a painful and slow growth; either way it is inevitable. Self must be sacrificed so that needs may be met and love may be expressed. This kind of love can also be felt for others, for the poor and needy, for our fellow believers, our family; as Paul felt for his own disciples:

"My dear children, for whom I am again in the pains of child-birth until Christ (Messiah) is formed in you, how I wish I could be with you now..." (Gal. 4:19-20)

Although we understand these principles when it comes to love of a human being, especially a child, we hardly think of applying them to a land, or a race of people. Yet this is exactly what the God of Israel does. Consider this key message:

> *"Is not Ephraim my dear son, the child in whom I delight?... my heart yearns for him like the yearning of a mother over her child."* (Jer. 31:20)

> *"How can I give you up, Ephraim? How can I hand you over, Israel?... My heart is changed within me; all my compassion is aroused."* (Hos. 11:8)

Chapter 3

Men ?

Although this book is written primarily for women,
some of its readers will be men. Such men are among
those who have a tender heart towards the work of
the Holy Spirit and are comfortable with the fact that
they will be a part of the Bride, the Lamb's wife. This
is because the Spirit's work is that of a mother. In
Biblical Hebrew God's Spirit (Ruach) is gramatically
feminine even though we call Holy Spirit male. The
Spirit is the ' , our advocate, one who
`comes alongside', one who supports, comforts,
encourages, sustains and helps us: for it is the
mother who is the primary symbol of comfort. What
better picture of comfort is there than that of an
infant suckling contentedly in mother's arms?
In a metaphorical sense, however, the Scriptures also
(amazingly) attribute the nursing role to men: *You
shall suck the milk of nations, you shall suck
the breast of kings."*(Is. 60:16a, R.S.V.)
Of course kings are men!! Therefore we know that
men too can fulfil this role! It is, however, primarily
the mother who, like the Holy Spirit, comes alongside
of the child - holding a hand as the first tentative
steps are taken, guiding the pencil as the first shaky
words are written, listening as the first simple words
are read. Mothers always continue to stand beside
their children; supporting a troubled teenager,

preparing a daughter for her wedding day, or helping care for the newly arrived grandchildren. This is because motherhood is a lifetime calling.

A mother never ceases to be a mother. Nothing, not even the death of a beloved only child, can take that experience away from her. However dimly, she will always bear in her mind the memory, in her heart the affection, and in her body the indelible marks of that experience which changed her life forever.

We live in an age of the unisex: unisex behaviour, unisex dress. Motherhood, however, is unique. Bizarre medical experimentation may succeed in achieving a male pregnancy, but this is foetus-incubation, not 'motherhood'.

There is equality in educational and employment opportunities. Equity is as it should be: although unfortunately homemaking and motherhood are often denigrated, and, in most parts of the world, women suffer markedly inferior status and treatment. In much of Africa, Asia and the Arab world, women are virtual slaves to father or husband; employed women are exploited and maltreated. In such societies girl babies are deliberately selected for abortion, infanticide is more likely to be perpetrated against girls, simply because they are female, young girls are 'sold' into marriage, or as beggars, prostitutes and sex-slaves and famous and wealthy men sexually exploit under-age girls. The international media hardly bothers with their plight, governments deliberately suppress the release of actual information, and, sadly, the male dominated Church is ignorant or asleep; or both. But these girls and women, also, were made in the Divine Image. They, too, were born to be complete and whole people: to fulfil their Divinely given potential.

Chapter 4

Eve

From the very beginning the woman was unique. The
creation of the entire universe remained unfinished
until she emerged. Only then was the Creator
satisfied, His work of creation complete.

Eve was created to become the mother of all the
living, (Gen. 3:20). Her name indicates this; it means
'living'. It was obviously not physically possible for
Eve to be the mother of all generations; but she was
the matriarch, the spiritual mother, just as Adam was
the father of us all (Rom. 4:16).

Our view of Eve has been tarnished by the role she
played in Adam's fall; but she was beautiful; perfect
in body, mind and spirit. She was perfectly equipped
for her role in the world of Eden, of paradise. Her
marriage with Adam, the perfect man and the perfect
husband, was idyllic. They were the perfect married
couple, but, interestingly, there has never been a
perfect human parent: Eve bore her first child after
'the fall.'

The role assigned to the newly created Eve was as
helper, lover and friend. Her role perfectly reflected,
in human form, the role of the Holy Spirit amongst
humanity: our comforter, supporter, helper and
friend. Eva was created as the human counterpart of
the 'Paraclete', the Counsellor, her oneness with
Adam was designed to be as the oneness within the

Godhead.

Chapter 5

Sarah, Rebekah and Rachel

<u>Sarah</u>

Sarah was the first who ever lived, the first righteous Jewish woman. In a mystical way her life birthed the possibility of the nation of Israel. When her life's work was completed, her death heralded the start of ongoing life for the nation: life of the people and life in the Land. There is a real sense in which the establishment of the State of Israel is a completion of the call of God upon Sarah's life.

Sarah's burial plot marks the first purchase of land in Israel. The cave of Macpelah was the first and only piece of his God-given inheritance in Eretz Israel that Abraham would ever own, a tiny down-payment on his inheritance.

This spot, scene of both religious co-existence and of bloodshed, is a symbol of Sarah's eternal influence upon the destiny of Israel, for both blessing and disaster. The repercussions of Sarah's single big mistake, her giving of her maid to Abraham, are still felt today. Ishmael was born of this union and the Arab peoples, the sons of Ishmael, are Hagar's descendants.

Although she was justified in doing so, Sarah's eventual rejection of Hagar's son as an appropriate companion for Isaac, separated the brothers, both physically and emotionally, even though Abraham loved them both. It has been a long and continuing alienation: but we must not forget that Abraham's fatherly heart-cry was: *"Oh that Ishmael would live in thy sight"* (Gen. 17:18)

Yet it was Sarah's need for a decent burial that spurred her husband to buy a territorial possession in the Land. Whereas the other sons were given gifts while Abrahan was still alive, Isaac inherited Abraham's entire estate (Gen. 25:5). Neither Isaac nor his descendants have ever revoked the ownership of the little burial plot at Hebron.

Although this burial site is now situated in the heavily Arab town of Hebron, the building upon it contains both a mosque and a synagogue, which is used on Sabbaths. Hebron attracts an earnest group of observant Jewish inhabitants. Despite the threat which a Palestinian land-authority may pose to their security, these dedicated Jews are determined to remain in their homes near Hebron, near the remains of their greatest forebears, Sarah and Abraham.

When their father, Abraham, the forefathers of the Jewish and Arab peoples, Isaac and Ishmael, cooperated together, setting a correct example of unity. They buried their father with his wife Sarah:

> *"Abraham...died at a good old age, an old man and full of years; and he was gathered to his people. His sons Isaac and Ishmael buried him in the cave of Machpelah near Mamre,... in the field Abraham had bought from the Hittites."*

(Gen. 25:9-11)

Sarah did not begin her faith journey as a woman of great faith, in fact she laughed at the promise of a son (Gen. 18:10) but she had no Bible to read and no religious education so she must not be judged. The heavenly visitor knew that she had laughed at his message but she was afraid and lied, denying her laughter, but he said, "*Yes, you did laugh*" (v.25). After the son, Isaac, was circumcised Sarah remembered the incident and no longer doubted, saying: "*God has brought me laughter, and everyone who hears about this will laugh with me. ...Who would have said to Abraham that Sarah would nurse children? Yet I have borne him a son in his old age.*" (Gen. 21:7)

<u>Rebekah</u>

Rebekah/Rebecca is one of the key matriarchs of Israel, the granddaughter of Abraham's brother (Gen. 24:48) and a beautiful woman whom Isaac loved as soon as he saw her. But she was a very flawed woman living within a family dynamic that was flawed. Although she had no children for the first twenty years of marriage she produced twin sons (Esau and Jacob): one for the father and one for the mother – favouritism which is always a mistake (Gen. 25:28).

When they were adults Rebekah assisted her favourite son, Jacob, to deceive his father into believing that he was his brother, Esau, and so he received the blessings of the firstborn. Esau was so enraged that Rebekah advised Jacob to flee to

Mesopotamia to her relatives there as Esau planned to kill him. She advised him to marry into the family because Esau's heathen wives caused her trouble. She told her husband, Isaac, that that was why Jacob had to go away. This was how and where Jacob met his two wives, Leah and Rachel, who were sisters, and their two female slaves, Bilhah and Zilpah: the four women who built up the house of Israel (Ruth 4:11).

<u>Rachel</u>

Sneaky tricks and deception featured also in the next generation of the Abrahamic family in that Jacob was forced by his uncle (Laban) to work for seven years for Rachel, the cousin whom he loved, only to discover that her older sister, Leah, had spent the wedding night in his bed (Gen. 29:16-28). His father-in-law expected another seven years of arduous toil in return for the hand of Rachel. Naturally there was rivalry between the sisters so that both handed over her slave-girl to bear children to Jacob on their behalf. Sarah had also once resorted to this custom, which had resulted in the birth of Ishmael to Sarah's Egyptian slave, Hagar.

Laban also used up his daughters' dowries and then treated them like foreigners (Gen. 31:15). Laban under-paid Jacob for 20 years, changed his wages ten times and tried to swindle him out of the livestock that he was accumulating through God's blessings. Relationships within the wider family became so hostile that Jacob took his large family and his stock and fled back towards home (v.17).

Although Laban did have knowledge of the God of Abraham and of his father Nahor it seems that monotheism was not as strong in the branch of the family that remained in Haran as in the branch in Canaan because Laban had household gods (v.34). It is not surprising that, for all her beauty moral principles were not deeply ingrained in Rachel. In fact she stole her father's idols when they escaped. Being furious, Laban pursued the escapees but Divine intervention prevented any conflict and Jacob and Laban made a covenant together before parting. Rachel lied to her father when he was searching all of Jacob's tents for the terrapin.

These idols were probably later buried by Jacob under an oak tree at Shechem (Nablus) (35:2-4) but Rachel had already died giving birth to her second son, Benjamin, who would be his father's favourite.

Plate 5.1. Rachel's Tomb near Bethlehem, Photo: D. Campbell, 1970.

The God of Abraham cared for Abraham's descendants and intervened, primarily giving the men guidance, help and protection throughout the generations but the women's role (although they wanted to be more than bit-players) was to be beautiful, to bear children and attract their husband's affection.

Chapter 6

Miriam and Her Mother Jocabed.

Much drama is implied in the simple narrative of Jocabed's successfully implemented plan to save her beautiful baby, Moses, from the fate which Pharaoh had decreed for all male Hebrew infants: a watery grave in the 'holy' River Nile. There was the drama of illegally concealing a baby for three months, the drama of planning a course of action, and, most of all there was the drama of carrying it out.

There are hidden messages in this story, of the pious devotion to the Lord of this Levitical couple, whose three children were destined for the strongest spiritual leadership of any siblings in all of Jewish history.

Hidden relationship issues are also present. Did the boy's father, Amran, grandson of Levi, know of his wife's plan? Perhaps not, but his oldest child, Miriam, certainly did. She was her mother's 'right hand man' and a key actress in the success of the venture.

Miriam had to be tutored in where to wait, what to say, and, more importantly, what not to say, and to whom.

What a heady responsibility for the young girl! We can imagine her suppressed excitement and trepidation as she watched none other than the pharaoh's daughter arrive to bathe, at the very spot where Moses' floating ark lay. Did the angels in

Heaven hold their breath as Miriam carried out her plan? We can imagine the joy with which she ran to get her mother, and the strain of presenting Jocabed to the princess as merely one of many possible Hebrew wet-nurses.

A special mother-daughter relationship of understanding, trust and mutual commitment is implied by the story. Miriam was an essential part of the plan. She and Jocabed were inter-dependent co-conspirators in a Divine rescue operation, although they may have had no inkling of the eternal significance of what they were undertaking.

Jocabed, whose Hebrew name probably means "*Y-h-w-h is glory*", had intense maternal love for her infant. This resolute love was not mere feeling, it entailed courage, and a commitment which resulted in action. Consequently redemption and deliverance were both the short-term and the long-term outcomes of Miriam's and Jocabed's combined and coordinated actions. The result was immediate deliverance for Moses when he was redeemed from the river and eventual redemption for the Hebrew people whom Moses helped to deliver from Egyptian bondage.

If this had been Miriam's only contribution to the survival and welfare of the Chosen People it would have earned her an honoured place in the Scriptures, but she played a vital support role in Moses' endeavours, and made some unique contributions of her own.

It is Miriam's song on the shores of the Red (Reed) Sea, which is the first record in Scripture of praise using dance:

"Then Miriam the prophetess, Aaron's sister, took the tambourine in her hand, and all the women followed her, with tambourines and dancing. Miriam sang to them: 'Sing to the Lord, for he is highly exalted. The horse and its rider he has hurled into the sea.'"

(Ex.15:20-21)

Rabbinic tradition indicates that Miriam was the wife of Caleb, and mother of Hur. This would account for Hur's role in assisting Aaron to lift Moses arms during the battle at Rephidim (Ex.17:12); however the Bible does not reveal whether Miriam was married or single. One may ask: if Miriam had never married, how could she be called a mother in Israel?

To answer this we refer to the story of Deborah. It was not Deborah's parental or marital status that was significant, but the quality of her commitment to the Lord, and her care of the people of Israel.

Miriam and Deborah were similar, in that Miriam possessed many of those attributes which earned Deborah the maternal title. Miriam, like Deborah after her, was a prophetess. She was also a leader, and not only of the women! All the people followed Miriam, even when her example was not what it should have been. Moses' very life, in babyhood, had been in her hands, as she kept a vigil by the Nile's reedy bank, and there was always a strong bond between her and both of her brothers, Aaron and Moses.

Although she was a prophetess in her own right, Miriam was strongly committed to both Moses and Aaron in their unique and demanding tasks as the Lord's spokesmen in Egypt, and amongst His people. Moses, for his part, was committed to his sister. He stood between her and the Lord's judgement of leprosy, when she and Aaron fell into sin, pleading: *"Oh God please heal her."* (Num.12:13)

Miriam set the people of Israel a primary example of praise and gratitude, by giving Him thanks and praise for His mighty acts on their behalf.

Chapter 7

Princess-Redeemer

One of the greatest unsung heroines of the Torah is the Egyptian princess, simply known as Pharoah's daughter. Being of the hated Egyptian race, and the daughter of one bent on murdering Jewish boys by sacrificing them to the Nile, the contribution of this young, presumably unmarried, woman is 'oft overlooked. This princess risked much to take Moses from the water, in violation of Pharoah's commands: she also risked much in taking him as her own child, knowing full-well his racial heritage.

> *"She saw the basket among the reeds and sent her slave girl to get it. She opened it and saw the baby. He was crying, and she felt sorry for him. 'This is one of the Hebrew babies,' she said." (Ex.2:5-6)*

Had she failed in compassion, had she withdrawn in fear, Moses, and many Hebrew slaves, perhaps the whole Jewish people, would have died; for genocide was Pharoah's avowed intent.

Moses first woman teacher was his Jewish mother. His second was his gentile adoptive mother, a woman of 'hesed', true benevolence and loving-kindness; one who had compassion on children, one of the first of the "righteous from among the nations" or righteous gentiles.

It was this woman who gave Moses both his name,

and the right to life without fear. When he was weaned she took him into her home, loved him, raised and educated him. Like many other righteous gentile women who risked much to succour Jewish children in times of persecution, such as during the Holocaust, when the call of his own people became strong, she had to relinquish him.

Chapter 8

Zipporah

Zipporah, the gentile wife of Moses, by saving her husband's life, kept open the way for the Exodus of the people of Israel, their deliverance from slavery in Egypt. Her actions helped to procure deliverance, salvation and redemption from bondage. Zipporah could have expected that her marriage and family life would be established with blood covenants; firstly in the redemption of a first born son by the exchange-sacrifice of two turtle doves, pigeons or lambs, and secondly in the circumcision of all of her sons.

Some commentators attribute the blame for Moses' son Gershon's uncircumcised state to Zipporah's objections or reluctance; but Scripture does not lay the blame at her feet. The Lord obviously regarded it as Moses' responsibility, as Moses was a son of the covenant. Certain death was His punishment for Moses' failure to implement the covenant of circumcision, the Eternal covenant of the Chosen People, for his son, in turn.
Moses' wife, Zipporah, with great courage and not a little anger, intervened. With rare spiritual insight this woman first perceived the problem and then acted to resolve it. Taking upon herself the role of the mo'hel she circumcised the child with a sharp flint knife.

Throwing the foreskin at Moses' feet she called him a
"*blood husband*", that is, a husband sealed in blood,
or redeemed with blood. This mother in Israel
delivered her husband's life, through the belated
entry of her son into the blood covenant of Israel.

(Ex. 2:21; 4:25; 18:2).

No matter how grim the circumstances, no matter
how dark the picture, the `mother in Israel' is not
content to simply trust. She is impelled to arise and
undertake concerted and decisive action. Many lie
down under their difficulties out of piety, resigned to
the unfathomable ways of Providence: whereas a
rising up, a preparedness to act, would enable them
to be overcomers and would eventually establish
them in hard won victory.

Chapter 9

<u>Rahab</u>

The Epistle to the Hebrews lists many of the Biblical giants of faith, those who changed world history by faith. By faith they conquered kingdoms, administered justice, shut the mouths of lions and escaped the edge of the sword. But there is only one woman in this list; only one female giant of faith, and she is set on a pedestal for the world to emulate - only one woman, the harlot, Rahab.

What an unlikely example to follow! Of all the matriarchs and godly women of the Scriptures she is the one so honoured. Esther, Rachel, Deborah and Hannah are not even mentioned, though they were indeed women of great faith. Sarah did warrant a mention, in parentheses as it were, as Abraham was the real giant of faith in their family's story. Yet, in the New Testament, Rahab, a gentile woman, and a woman with a sinful past, is honoured, and her faith is praised.

Perhaps this is because the Jewish matriarchs were expected to be godly and faith-filled, while Rahab was the most unlikely candidate for holiness. Rahab, who, like Mary Magdalene, from whom seven demons had been cast (`though Mary was not a prostitute), had been delivered from much, therefore gave much devotion and love.

Rahab was not only a gentile, she was a pagan, and

one of the enemy, one of the dreaded Canaanites, a 'mere' woman, and socially from the bottom echelons of her society. Yet by faith she became an Israelite, a godly wife and the mother of Boaz, whom we know of as a righteous man. By faith Rahab received her place in the royal family of David, and the Messianic lineage of Y'shuah, Jesus from Nazareth.

It seems that Rahab was a particularly spiritually sensitive person, as she alone in Jericho discerned that the great God of heaven and earth was with Israel, and would assist them in the coming battle. By faith Rahab and her family trusted in the word of honour of the spies, and also in Joshua's willingness to honour the oath which the spies had sworn:

> "' *Our liver for your lives,' the man assured her,*
> *'If you don't tell what we are doing, we will*
> *treat you kindly and faithfully when the Lord*
> *gives us the land.'*" (Josh. 2:14)

While previously Rahab would have welcomed the spies as potential clients, she laid aside her base motives and risked her life for them. Was this because they paid her well? No! It was because of the conviction of her heart: because she caught a glimpse of the Eternal One and was able to lay 'Self' aside: self-gratification, self-seeking and even self-preservation.

Through Sarah's faith Israel was born. Through Rahab's faith Israel was victorious at Jericho and gained a first foothold possession in their Promised

Land. This was part of a great plan to fulfil Jacob's desire for his people to return to their Land, and God's promises to Abraham:

> "Know for certain that your descendants will
> be strangers in a country not their own and
> they will be enslaved and ill-treated four
> hundred years... In the fourth generation your
> descendants will come back here... To your
> descendants I will give this land."
>
> (Gen. 15:13 & 18)

Rahab's family consisted of her mother, father, sisters, and brothers, and all who belonged to them, (Josh. 2:12). She was a gentile and had neither children nor husband, yet she was a mother-in-Israel. Her assistance provided vital physical protection for the people of Israel, and she helped them to possess their inheritance, the soil of Eretz Israel. Both her spiritual insights and practical action opened the way for the prophetic word of the Lord to come to pass. So too, today, mental assent about Israel's right to the Land, even deep conviction, is not enough. Faith without works is dead. Rahab possessed a quality blend of conviction and action, praised even centuries later:

> *"Was not even Rahab the prostitute considered
> righteous for what she did when she gave
> lodging to the spies and sent them off in a
> different direction?"* (Jas. 2:25)

<u>The Scarlet Thread</u>

By faith Rahab trusted in the scarlet thread which she
tied in her window. What some consider the sign of
her `profession', became a message to her deliverer,
to Joshua, whose very name means `saviour'. By
faith Rahab trusted in the scarlet thread. By
remaining within the house upon which a Divine
pledge rested, she and her family were delivered
from death.

Similarly another scarlet thread had brought
deliverance when the children of Israel were in the
midst of a strange and alien people. In Egypt the
scarlet blood of the Passover Lamb upon the
doorframes saved all those in the house, they
escaped death on that first Passover night. This
Passover event was established by the same hallowed
principle:

"*You hall be saved and your whole* household." (Acts 16:31)
As it was in Egypt on the eve of the Exodus, so it was
in Jericho: any member of Rahab's family who left her
house would have come out from under the
guarantee of protection.

For centuries, Israel, like us, lived under a seal of
blood, a seal given to forgive sin; "*For without the
shedding of blood there is no forgiveness.*"

(Heb. 9:22)

The interpretation of Rahab's scarlet thread as symbolic of blood is of great antiquity, having been taught by Justin Martyr, Irenaeus and Clement of Rome. A few decades after St Paul's martyrdom in Rome, in his First Epistle to the Corinthians (XII), Bishop Clement wrote:

<u>The Scapegoat</u>

Each year on Yom Kippur, the Day of Atonement, as the High Priest sacrificed the goat, Israel experienced a deliverance from death, the punishment for sin, via a scarlet stream of blood. This blood was symbolised by yet another scarlet thread, the one tied upon the head of a second and identical goat, the goat known as the ' scapegoat'. Whilst the first goat was sacrificed, and its blood sprinkled upon the Mercy Seat, within the Holy of Holies, (that is, upon the covering of the Ark of the Covenant) the accumulated guilt of the sins of all Israel was placed upon the head of the second goat. This goat, with scarlet chord still upon it, was then expelled from the camp, sent into the wilderness, perhaps to die.

> *"He (the High Priest) shall bring forward the live goat. He is to lay both hands on the head of the live goat and confess over it all the wickedness and rebellion of the Israelites - all their sins - and put them on the goat's head. He shall send the goat away into the desert in the care of a man appointed for the task. The goat will carry on itself all their sins to a solitary place; and the man shall release it in*

the desert. (Lev. 16:20b-22)

There is a scarlet blood drenched thread of deliverance throughout Scripture, running continuously through both Testaments, demonstrating the continuity of the revelation, from the one to the other. It runs from Abel's righteous blood-sacrifice to the first Passover deliverance in Egypt, and on and on. It continues on, into Israel's future, when a fountain will be opened to the house

of David to cleanse from sin and iniquity. The blood, sprinkled or poured in the Temple sacrificial system, the blood of each scapegoat and the blood of each red heifer; all are parts of this deliverance.

<u>The Red Heifer</u>

As often as was necessary the High Priest, the Cohen Hagadol, sacrificed and then burnt an unblemished red heifer on the Mount of Olives. The animal was burnt with scarlet cloth and the red wood of the hyssop bush. From the ashes of this fire the `water of cleansing' was made, for use in ritual purifications. If ever Israel is to have a Third Temple, such water will again be needed to purify the Temple area, as well as the future priests, the cohenim of Israel, and the Temple implements and furnishings, as well as the sanctuary itself. Up until this week no such red heifer was available although a worldwide search had been made for decades. This week, however, five red heifers arrived in Israel from Texas and were declared to be "without blemish" by the appropriate Jewish authorities.

The scarlet symbols, a red heifer, red fabric and red

wood, denoted blood: blood sacrifice. Each time they were used they prefigured a blood sacrifice in which all the world would one day come to trust.

According to the Scriptural theme of the scarlet thread, its significant message will terminate in the land of Israel, after the last battle:

> *"Who is this coming from Edom, from Bozrah,*
> *with his garments stained crimson? Who is*
> *this, robed in splendour, striding forward in the*
> *greatness of his strength? 'It is I speaking in*
> *righteousness, mighty to save.' Why are your*
> *garments red like those of one treading the*
> *winepress? I have trodden the winepress*
> *alone; from the nations no-one was with me. I*
> *trampled them in my anger and trod them*
> *down in my wrath, their blood spattered my*
> *garments, and I stained all my clothing."*

(Is. 63:1-3)

Who is this? It is Messiah in judgement, blood stained from the battle, yet victorious.

It is, therefore, no accident that Rahab and her family sheltered under a scarlet chord as she trusted in the word of the servants of the God of Israel. The spies word was trustworthy and Rahab's family was saved. Joshua permitted her to live amongst the tribes, and, by implication, to marry into Israel. Rahab did indeed so marry, and gave birth to Boaz, who married Ruth the Moabitess.

In this respect, Rahab, like her gentile daughter-in-law, Ruth, is the spiritual mother of all those who

have been adopted by Israel's God, as sons and
daughters of Abraham, accepted into the family of
Jesus (Y'shuah), as his brothers and sisters, and
gathered into the Commonwealth of Israel.

Chapter 10

Naomi and Ruth

<u>Naomi</u>

In an early `diaspora' Naomi was cut off from her Land and her people, widowed and deprived of both her children. She is often thought of as a bitter woman, because she returned from Moab to Israel bitter in spirit. She was painfully aware of her inner distress, asking to be called Mara (`bitter'), rather than Naomi (`pleasant').

Yet this was only one aspect, a temporary aspect, of Naomi's personality. Both of Naomi's daughters-in-law, Orpah and Ruth, loved her, weeping repeatedly when they came to the place of parting. To have been thus loved, Naomi, a devoted wife and mother, must also have been a gracious and caring mother-in-law. It was Naomi's love for the two young women which motivated her to send them back to their parent's home. It was a love that wanted to see them happily remarried. Although she needed them she put their welfare before her own, and was willing to set out on her journey through the wilderness of Judea, desolate and alone.

Naomi's bitterness was healed as she returned to her Land, her people, and her village. She also returned to her own possession, her own little piece of the soil of Israel. She not only returned to her own inheritance, but she was blessed in the arduous and dangerous journey by the support of Ruth, who loved her with a staunch devotion.

<u>Ruth</u>

Naomi loved Ruth: loved her as her own flesh and blood, always calling her "my daughter". It was, therefore, not long after the home-coming that Naomi's bitterness waned and she was able to say:

> *"The Lord has not stopped showing his*
> *kindness to the living and the dead."*

(Ruth 2:20)

Once they were settled in Bethlehem, Naomi carefully tutored Ruth in the customs of this strange culture, so that Ruth neither ruined their reputations nor cruelled her chance of remarriage. Naomi behaved as a good Jewish momma. She was a perceptive and astute matchmaker, with real insight into the ways of men.

The book of Ruth is clearly a love story between a man and a woman - meeting, courtship, marriage and the establishment of a family - a familiar and unremarkable pattern. The story is a little unusual in that Boaz was, presumably, still a bachelor - unusual considering his mature years and considerable affluence, while Ruth was already a widow and perhaps not so young. Ruth was hardly the ideal bride: she was childless despite about ten years of marriage, not to mention the fact that she was an alien - a foreigner and a gentile.

Another of Naomi's closest kinsmen had declined to marry Ruth, fearing to endanger his inheritance -

perhaps he meant the rights of previous children, but more likely he feared endangering his status by marrying an alien.

For Boaz this was hardly a problem, he himself was the son of a 'mixed marriage', as his mother was Rahab. With such a heritage Boaz would have understood that, if she was willing, a God-fearing and virtuous gentile woman could become a devoted daughter of Israel. Boaz was able to comprehend the desire of Ruth's heart.

'Ruth' is also a love story on two other levels, one fairly obvious and another deeper, more hidden. The relationship between Naomi and Ruth is of paramount significance as theirs is the Bible's premier example of a relationship between two women, explained in depth. Despite their age difference and racial difference Ruth and Naomi contradict the notion that daughters-in-law are 'outsiders'. Their hearts were as one.

Christians generally do not understand the significance of the distinction between Ruth and Naomi, both are simply Biblical heroines, but Jewish people cannot escape the distinction. Ruth is called 'Ruth the convert', her gentile racial heritage is inescapable, her conversion from paganism to Judaism her most notable feature.

Christians often interpret Naomi as emblematic of the Land of Israel, the land to which she dreamed of returning even though she was widowed and bereaved of her sons. Ruth is a foreigner, a gentile, who, never the less, dedicates herself to serving Israel and worshipping the God of Israel.

Naomi was a mother in Israel because of her care and compassion, her love for Ruth and the great care she lavished upon the baby Ruth bore. So great was Naomi's maternal care and devotion to this child that the women of Bethlehem said: "Naomi has a son." (Ruth 4:17)

This son, so welcome and so loved, had a significant Messianic role. He was to be King David's grandfather.

Had the love between Ruth and Naomi not been strong Ruth would never have accompanied her to Bethlehem. If Naomi's example had not awakened within Ruth a desire to know the God of Israel, Ruth would not have willingly left her own race and her own family, to join herself to Israel. Had Ruth not loved Naomi, Ruth would not have affirmed:

> *"Your people will be my people and your God my God."* (Ruth 1:16)

As her reward, Ruth was provided with a good husband, and a son, although she had borne no children to her first husband, Mahlon. Through the birth of this child she also joined herself to the royal and Messianic line of Judah.

In the distant and foreign land of Moab, Naomi chose to love her gentile daughter-in-law and so Naomi kindled devotion. This devotion was returned to

Naomi many times over: so much so that everyone acknowledged that this foreign woman, this gentile, was better to Naomi than seven sons. What an amazing commendation in a Jewish community! Orpah is always pictured with her back to Naomi, walking away, yet Naomi

commended her to the God of Israel (Ruth 1:8).

Ruth is often pictured clinging to Naomi or embracing her. In the story there is a little phrase, such an understatement of the closeness of their bond, the unity of their purpose and the difficulties they faced in the journey:

> "*And they went, both of them, until they came to Bethlehem*." (Ruth 1:19)

Naomi was a true 'mother in Israel', even in distant Moab, because she kept alive her love for Israel. She kept alive her commitment to the God of Israel, even in the most adverse of circumstances. In the midst of her pain and bereavement Naomi dared to love others, even gentiles.

Chapter 11

Deborah, Jael and Judith

<u>Deborah</u>

It was the prophetess Deborah who first used the term `a mother in Israel'. In fact she used it of herself, in a song of great antiquity; a song which bears the hallmarks of female composition, expressing events and feelings through female eyes (even expressing some sympathy for the mother of her slain enemy). Here is the primary reference:

"In the days of Shamgar son of Anath, in the days of Jael, the roads were abandoned; travellers took to winding paths. Village life in Israel ceased, ceased until I, Deborah, arose, arose a mother in Israel."

(Jud. 5:6-7)

Deborah, we read, was the wife of Lappidoth. She was a `judge', that is to say a magistrate and ruler in Israel. This was a time of spiritual decay in Israel, during which time, for twenty years, Israel was in bondage to the Canaanites. These were a cruel but powerful people who possessed superior technology: iron chariots, and 900 of them at that!

Deborah was a wise, courageous and godly woman. Despite Israel's state of apostasy, the people turned to the Lord for help and deliverance; an outcome which was presumably attributable to Deborah's influence. She was a true prophetess who had great authority. We know, for example, that the General, Barak, recognised her authority; Barak, the commander of all the armed men of the tribes of Zebulun and Naphtali

!

Barak agreed to fight the Canaanites near Megiddo, but only if Deborah would accompany him. Perhaps his need for her presence was as much an acknowledgment of the anointing that rested upon her as an expression of any fear of doing the job alone.

The Bible does not suggest that Deborah's leadership was a mistake, nor that it had only been possible because the men were too weak to take on the role. Rather it indicates that she was respected. The people looked to her for leadership, and they willingly volunteered to follow her. Only honour is laid by the Scriptures at Deborah's feet. While soldiers from the tribe of Issachar assisted those normally under Barak's command, the tribes that didn't assist Deborah wished that they had (Jud. 5:13-17).

We know that Deborah was a true prophetess as her prophesies came to pass.

Two key aspects were fulfilled, in detail.

(1) The army of Sisera was given into Israel's hands, in accordance with her words:

> *"The Lord, the God of Israel, commands you:*
> *'Go take with you ten thousand men of*
> *Naphtali and Zebulun and lead the way to*
> *Mount Tabor. I will lure Sisera, the commander*

*of Jabin's army, with his chariots and his
troops to the Kishon River and give him into
your hands".* (Jud. 4:7)
Secondly, the honour of killing Sisera was given, not
to Barak, the commander, but to a woman, Jael; just
as Deborah foretold: "*The honour will not be
yours, for the Lord will hand Sisera over to a
woman.*" (Jud. 4:9)
Deborah's prophesy of Sisera's defeat came to pass
when a cloud-burst trapped the iron chariots and
washed many away in the river. Jael, the second
heroine of this story, rounded off the Canaanite
defeat by taking Sisera's life, after he fled from the
battlefield. This woman's achievement was extolled
by Deborah in song:

> "*Most blessed of women be Jael, the wife of
> Heber the Kenite, most blessed of tent-
> dwelling women. He (Sisera) asked for water
> and she gave him milk; in a bowl fit for nobles
> she gave him curdled milk. Her hand reached
> for the tent peg, her right hand for the
> workman's hammer. She struck Sisera, she
> crushed his head, she shattered and pierced
> his temple. At her feet he sank, he fell, there he
> lay.*" (Jud. 4:24-27a)

Deborah was jubilant about what she and Jael had
accomplished, yet she was humble. She accorded
honour to Barak, perhaps more than he deserved:
but it was to Lord, the One of Sinai, the God of Israel,
that she, like Miriam before her, sang her song of

praise:

> *"Hear this, you kings! Listen you rulers! I will*
> *sing to the Lord, I will sing; I will make music*
> *to the Lord the God of Israel."* (Jud. 5:3)

Deborah's song of praise has definite overtones of Miriam's earlier song of deliverance from the army of Egypt. This is not surprising, given the similarities in the acts of deliverance, which the Lord performed in each case. On both occasions, enemy armies, chariots and all, were swept away in floods of water.

In what way was Deborah a mother in Israel? Unquestionably she was guided by the Spirit of the Lord. She heard from the Lord, and she fearlessly conveyed His message, even to the highest men in the land. She even required that kings listen to her words! (Foreign kings - because this was before Israel's monarchy existed.) She clearly saw the spiritual condition into which Israel had fallen, and was prepared to risk her physical safety in order to strengthen the army. She was motivated by a spirit of altruism and self-sacrifice, which lies at the heart of motherhood.

Although she was humble, Deborah was forthright, a woman of faith and a true and effective encourager. Before the battle she urged Barak forward, with assurance:

> *"Then Deborah said to Barak, 'Go! This is the*
> *day the Lord has given Sisera into your hands.*
> *Has not the Lord gone ahead of you?'"*

(Jud. 4:14)

Deborah knew the importance of action: in the day of trouble she arose! She knew the importance of the contribution of willing volunteers, especially when they are directed by good leaders.

Twice in her victory song she paid tribute to the people who willingly offered themselves; and her heart was with them. Finally, and most significantly, she knew that the victory came from the hand of the God of Israel, and she gave Him the honour and the praise.

While Joshua was still alive, the angel of the Lord had promised Israel peace from their enemies, but only while they walked in the ways of their God, (Jud. 2:1-4). Keeping Israel on this path was a chief function of the judges.

Whilst a judge lived, he, or she, saved the children of Israel out of their enemies' hands and the Lord had compassion on them. Upon the death of each judge the people usually fell into greater corruption and paganism than before, with consequent Divine punishment (See Jud.2:18-19).Deborah was a judge and while she lived she led Israel in peace for over forty years. That peace is the sign that, under her leadership, the people served the Lord Almighty. While ever she lived Deborah turned Israel's hearts unto their God. Deborah displayed a motherly concern for ongoing village life, for community life.

She could clearly see the detrimental effects of the enemy's interference with the normal functioning of commerce, trades, travel, plus the social contacts of marriage, friendship and kinship. The need to end this interference is what inexorably motivated her into action.

Deborah was diligent and forthright. Deborah, a true mother in Israel, displayed an exceptional blend of spiritual, moral and physical strength, courage, faith and commitment. Finally, like Miriam, Deborah understood that Israel belonged to the God of Israel, for ever.

Jael

Jael had physical and mental strength. Her name means 'wild goat' and she lived up to her name in that her barbaric deed in driving a tent peg through the temple of an arch-enemy, after having deceived him into accepting her hospitality, was certainly wild for a woman and she was no sheep.

Plate 11.1. Bedouin tent such as Jael lived in.
Photo: D. Campbell, 1988.

At this time Israel had long been under the thumb of

the Canaanite peoples and King Jabin, who was based in Hazor, and Jael's courageous, even daring act, coupled with Barak's victory in battle, brought deliverance from them (Jud. 5:31b).

<u>Judith</u>

During the Feast of Hanukkah, yet another woman, Judith, is honoured. Judith's story is found in the Apocrypha, which is not accepted as canonical by Protestants, but that does not mean that its narratives are untrue. It is, in fact, good information from between the period of the Old and New Testaments: the Inter-Testamental Period.

Judith's contribution to the welfare of Israel was in the spirit of Miriam, Deborah, Ruth and Jael. Like Deborah she was an encourager; and an exhorter, even of the men in the civil and military leadership. Like Hulda she was a prophetess to whom the city leaders came for counsel, saying:

"All that thou hast spoken hast thou spoken with a good heart, and there is none that shall gainsay thy words. For this is not the first day wherein thy wisdom is manifested; but from the beginning of thy days all people have known thy understanding, because the disposition of thy heart is good."

(Judith 8:28-9)

Like Deborah, Judith was a woman of action, and like Ruth, and the later prophetess, Anna, she was a virtuous and godly widow, given to prayer and fasting. Like Jael, she single handedly killed an enemy leader, having tempted him to his death with her wiles. In the footsteps of Miriam she led the people of Israel in joyful dance of thanksgiving with timbrels. Like both Deborah and Miriam she composed songs of praise:

"Begin unto my God with timbrels, Sing unto my Lord with cymbals; Tune unto him psalm and praise; Exalt him and call upon his name."

Judith

During the Feast of Hanukkah, yet another woman, Judith, is honoured. Judith's story is found in the Apocrypha, which is not accepted as canonical by Protestants, but that does not mean that its narratives are untrue. It is, in fact, good information from between the period of the Old and New Testaments: the Inter-Testamental Period. Judith's contribution to the welfare of Israel was in the spirit of Miriam, Deborah, Ruth and Jael. Like Deborah she was an encourager; and an exhorter, even of the men in the civil and military leadership. Like Hulda she was a prophetess to whom the city leaders came for counsel, saying:

> "All that thou hast spoken hast thou spoken with a good heart, and there is none that shall gainsay thy words. For this is not the first day wherein thy wisdom is manifested; but from the beginning of thy days all people have known thy understanding, because the disposition of thy heart is good."
>
> (Judith 8:28-9)

Like Deborah, Judith was a woman of action, and like Ruth, and the later prophetess, Anna, she was a virtuous and godly widow, given to prayer and fasting. Like Jael, she single handedly killed an enemy leader, having tempted him to his death with her wiles. In the footsteps of Miriam she led the people of Israel in joyful dance of thanksgiving with timbrels. Like both Deborah and Miriam she composed songs of praise:

> "*Begin unto my God with timbrels, Sing unto my Lord with cymbals; Tune unto him psalm and praise; Exalt him and call upon his name.*"

(Judith 16:2)

One of the greatest contributions of women in ancient Israel was through playing music, singing and dancing: not of a secular kind but in praise and worship. The figurine in Plate 11.2 was found in Isdrael and is one of many similar female musicians there.

Chapter 12

<u>Hannah</u>

Hannah, and the matriarch Rachel, were their husband's favourite wives. Like Rachel, Hannah was
not only childless, but scorned by the other wife. Hannah's husband, Elkanah, like Rachel's husband Jacob, was not perturbed by the barrenness of his favourite wife. Both men's love was independent of the woman's childbearing role. Each had a second wife and could also father children by many women, as Jacob did, but they were able to have that certain exceptional relationship only with the beloved wife. Despite the love and devotion shown to them by their husbands, both women felt keenly the social reproach of their condition, and the pain of their own misfortune, their lack.

Elkanah, for his part, attempted to console Hannah, saying:

"Hannah, why are you weeping? Why don't you eat?
Why are you downhearted? Don't I mean more
to you than ten sons?

(I Sam.1:8)

Clearly Hannah's husband was no substitute for children, and the status they would bring to her in the face of the other wife's scorn. Neither was his love adequate balm for the deep anguish of her soul. This was a spiritual wound, deeper than a mere man could heal. Fortunately for her health, and for Israel's good,

Hannah knew Whom to seek.

She brought her need to the Lord, to the very door of His resting place, the place where the Ark of His Presence sheltered, in the

Tabernacle at Shiloh. Her prayer to the Lord there was:

> *"O Lord Almighty, if you will only look upon*
> *your servant's misery and remember me, and*
> *not forget your servant but give her a son, then*
> *I will give him to the Lord for all the days of his*
> *life, and no razor will ever be used on his*
> *head." (I Sam.1:11)*

It might seem that Hannah had been blessed with almost everything that she could have wanted, a happy marriage with a good and loving husband, a satisfying and shared religious devotion. Her husband obviously had sufficient wealth to travel at will, and to provide the necessary animal sacrifices. Yet her grief could not be consoled, until the High Priest's prayer poured balm - shalom from the Lord - into her heart. The worship she offered next morning, before returning home, was from a joyful heart. Her life, her expectations and her attitudes had been totally and instantly transformed.

Hannah's life was soon to be radically changed yet again, when, at last, she gave birth to the son for whom she had beseeched the Lord. In her joy, however, she did not forget the miracle that had been provided, nor the vow she had made, to give the child back to the Lord.

Meanwhile her ever-loving husband permitted her to do whatever seemed right to her, while encouraging her to keep her vow.

Hannah's sacrifice, in giving her newly weaned child to the Lord, for perpetual service in the Tabernacle, is almost too traumatic to comprehend. How this loving mother could surrender him to the aged priest, Eli, is unfathomable.

Undoubtedly Hannah refrained from weaning Samuel for as long as was possible, but there is no hint of resistance in her self-sacrifice. She had made a covenant with her God and, because He had been found faithful, she would also be faithful.

What a gift she gave: Samuel became a prophet, a military leader, a judge and perhaps a priest and he reluctantly anointed Saul as king and later willingly, although secretly, anointed David as king and oversaw the transition to the monarchy.

Chapter 13

<u>Huldah</u>

As we climb the Huldah Steps, those ancient and time-worn steps external to the southern wall of Jerusalem's Temple Mount, up to the sealed arches of the Huldah Gates, some understanding of the little known figure of Huldah may emerge from the misty past. How unusual, we may ponder, that this once grand and expansive staircase should have been named for an almost unknown woman, and one who had been dead for almost six hundred years before these steps were constructed.

The Huldah Stairs are authentic remains from the last Temple, and were designed to provide access, via the Huldah Gates, to underground stairs and the passageways that which surfaced in Herod's Royal Stoa and guest quarters.

An examination of the scale-model of Jerusalem, as it existed in the early first century, after Herod's restoration of the Temple, can provide information about this staircase. The model, originally in the grounds of the Holyland Hotel but now at the Israel Museum, shows that, by the first century, Huldah's monument (or perhaps her tomb) had long been situated nearby, to the south of Temple Mount - hence the name of the stairs. Great respect is indicated by its position.

We must turn to the Tanach for further clues on this

intriguing matter. It was during the reign of Josiah, King of Judah, in about 622 B.C.E., that Hilkiah the High Priest discovered the Book of the Law in the Temple. This scroll was read in King Josiah's presence and he became so convicted of sin that he tore his robes in repentance. The king longed for a fresh and personal word from the Lord, a reassurance of the meaning of what had been read to him.
He issued the royal command:

"Go and inquire of the Lord for me and for the people." (II Kng. 22:13)

The high priest and court servants knew whom to ask. Without dissension or hesitation they sought out the prophetess Huldah at her home in Jerusalem's second district or college. Huldah, an acknowledged and respected prophetess, was the wife of Shallum, of the family who, by tradition, cared for the Temple garments.

In this respect Huldah resembled Judith, whose story is told in the Book of Judith. Even kings and priests knew who would deal honestly and righteously with their request for Divine guidance. The lives of both Huldah and Judith had obviously been of such godly calibre that their status as the oracles of the Lord was unquestioned.

Even though Huldah's prophetic message was one of doom and judgement the king was neither angry nor dismayed. Having his convictions confirmed by Huldah, he increased in zeal for purity and godliness, and embarked upon a campaign of spiritual and ritual cleansing throughout the land.

A royal revival was instigated throughout Jerusalem and Judah. Altars to idols were smashed and desecrated, Asherah groves and phallic stele were smashed, the Temple quarters of male prostitutes were destroyed, the priests of idolatry were killed, along with mediums and spiritists. Religious artefacts were burned, and all household gods and idols were removed.

The pinnacle of this process was the desecration of the site where Molech had been worshipped. Here Hebrew parents had sacrificed their children in the flames of idolatry, here God's sacred commandments had been flagrantly flouted, the gift of children cruelly destroyed.

This cleansing was followed by the public reading of the Torah, with fervour. A wonderful renewal of the eternal covenant between God and Israel occurred:

> *"The king stood by the pillar and renewed the*
> *covenant in the presence of the Lord - to follow*
> *the Lord and keep his commands, regulations*
> *and decrees, with all his heart and all his soul."*

(II Kng. 23:3)

The renewed religious devotion expressed itself in renewed commitment to the covenant by both king and people; as well as renewed dedication to celebrating the feasts of Israel. They immediately began with a wholehearted Passover celebration:

> *"Not since the days of the judges who led*
> *Israel and the kings of Judah, had any such*

Passover been observed." (II Kng. 23:22)

The direct result of the ministry of this mother-in-
Israel was a spiritual deliverance and restoration. This
revival did not, however, avert the judgement which
Huldah had foretold, but King Josiah, who was
unequalled in zeal for the Lord, died in battle. He was
spared the experience of the disgrace that awaited
his kingdom.
The foretold punishment came about in 586 B.C.E.,
Josiah's death, when Nebuchadnezzar besieged and
captured Jerusalem and placed Zedekiah on the
throne as a puppet. When Zedekiah rebelled
Jerusalem was besieged and captured (Jer. 52:6-7).
Solomon's beautiful Temple was burned and the
Temple treasures were removed to Babylon, along
with King Zedekiah and all inhabitants except the very
poorest agricultural workers of the land (II King.
25:4-7; 10; 17-20).

Plate 13.1. The Huldah Steps when first excavated. Photo: D. Campbell, 1988.

Chapter 14

The Mother of Samson the Nazarite

The chief characteristic of the Nazarite in ancient
Israel was that he, or she, was set apart to God - the
title being taken from the Hebrew word `nazir',
meaning separated or consecrated. It included either
a permanent or a temporary consecration. The
separation was a God-given provision for men or
women who wished to make a special commitment or
vow to the Lord, which, in the majority of cases was a
temporary vow. This is outlined in Num. 6:1-21.
The Mishna (in Nazir 3:6) even records such a vow,
made by a woman proselyte to Judaism, Queen-
mother Helena, the mother of the king of Adiabene,
from beyond the Tigris River. The Jewish historian,
Josephus, recorded that she visited Jerusalem to
bring financial gifts, (and probably to fulfil her vow in
the Temple).
From Moses' day onwards, unshaven and uncut hair
was defined as the sign of the Nazarite.

> *"The symbol of his separation to God is on his
> head."* (I Sam. 6:7)

The cutting of his nails and the shaving off and
burning of the hair, in the fire of the altar of sacrifice,
was the sign that the Nazarite's vow had been
fulfilled: whereas the sign of life-long dedication to

the Lord, of perpetual Nazariteship, was that no razor
was ever to be used upon the head or body. The long
hair was a constant reminder, both to the Nazarite
and to the people of Israel, of his, or indeed her,
calling. Similarly no grapes (which may have begun to
ferment), nor products of the vine, nor alcohol, were
to be consumed.

Also, no ritually unclean items were to be touched,
not even the corpse of an immediate family member.
This was a requirement stricter than that of a priest,
and equal with that of the High Priest. Any such
contamination would exclude the high priest from
participating in the ritual and worship of the Lord; it
would temporarily cut him off, as it were, from the
house of Israel: a situation to be painstakingly
avoided. Similarly the Nazarite was to be constantly
available as the Lord's servant.

As the chosen or voluntary servant of Adoni it was
imperative that the Nazarite, also, remain in intimate
fellowship with YHWH. Everything that might mar this
open relationship was to be scrupulously avoided.
Because of its attendant loss of inhibitions, the
Nazarite was to abstain from alcohol, lest he more
easily fall into sin.

So strong was the expediency for Samson to be
separate, dedicated to the Lord, and kept apart from
spiritual and ritual uncleanness, that the requirements
of a Nazarite were imposed, by an angelic
messenger, upon Samson's mother even before he
was conceived.

Both of Samson's parents knew that their son was to
have an exceptional upbringing and a unique task in
life; the task of Israel's deliverer. Both of them knew
the messages from the angelic messenger and both
consented to this plan. Even though they knew that it
would be a challenge, both resolved to fulfil its
requirements exactly:

> *"Manoah prayed to the Lord: 'O Lord, I beg*
> *you, let the man of God you sent to us come*
> *again to teach us how to bring up the boy who*
> *is to be born.'"* (Jud. 13:8)

At the time of this prayer only Manoah's wife had
seen the seraph, and it was to her, the mother-to-be,
that the angelic visitor appeared the second time, in
response to Manoah's prayer. It was God's priority
that the mother understand exactly the details of the
plan. Even though her name is not given, this saga is
Samson's mother's story, as Samson's uniqueness
was primarily a covenant agreement between her and
the Lord.

Jewishness today is defined by the religion of the
maternal line. Hassidic Judaism teaches that this is
because of the prime significance of the mother's
role: as the one who transmits to each Jewish child its
`Jewish soul' and teaches the basic principles of faith
and fear of God. It is said that these significant tasks
are Divinely conferred because women are innately
more spiritually sensitive, and have higher levels of
faith than men. This was certainly true in the case of
Samson's mother.

Although, punitively, the role of women in the Scriptural accounts is not great, they have a profound qualitative importance. Women entered the narrative at crisis points. Women were involved in prophetic, dramatic and vital events, at times when, often, Israel's future hung in the balance. Women performed their contribution to acts of deliverance unwaveringly, with great perseverance. Successful, though somewhat unsung, they then withdrew from centre stage, often disappearing into the unknown from whence they had come. Samson's mother was such a woman.

This dedicated and faithful woman, Manoah's wife, was a person of significant spiritual insight. She knew immediately that the messenger was an angel sent from God. This fact was the very first thing that she told her husband. By contrast Manoah did not realise it until much later, after the angel's miraculous disappearance in the flames of the sacrifice they offered. Also, it was she who assuaged Manoah's fears, assuring him that God would not have revealed these matters to them if He intended to kill them for having seen His face.

It is interesting that, despite Samson's well-known deviations from the pre-ordained path of righteousness, God was with him (Jud. 15:18f). This should not surprise us, however, because the angel had promised his mother, from On High, that: "The boy will be a Nazarite of God from birth until the day of his death." (Jud. 13:7)

This promise accords with the teaching that God does not regret and retract His call upon lives, nor the gifts He has given. The Nazarite calling remained upon Samson's life despite his behaviour. It is fitting that, between the Passover crucifixion and the Day of Pentecost, all the disciples continually gathered for prayer in an upper room, with Mary, a unique 'mother in Israel':

> *"They all joined together constantly in prayer, along with the women and Mary, the mother of Jesus, and his brothers."* (Act. 1:14)

Chapter 15

<u>Abigail</u>

Abigail's narrative is found in I Sam. 25:2ff. She is
one of the biblical heroines whose name is known:
Abigail means 'my father is joy'. When her narrative
begins she is the wife of a surly and mean, but
wealthy, husband called Nabal, which means 'fool'
or 'folly'.

Abigail was a woman of both determination and
humility. She is shy and yet iron-willed, meek and yet
fearless, quiet and yet forthright with excellent verbal
skills. She had been a devoted wife to her crass
husband, Nabal, and in widowhood, to her second
husband, King David.

Abigail had beauty, dignity, charm, wit, wisdom and
verbal fluency. In an era when women were married
shortly after puberty and expected to be quietly
preoccupied with onerous and arduous household
chores, such as grinding wheat, baking bread,
making olive oil, spinning and weaving, Abigail took
a great risk is acting contrary to Nabal's clear
intentions.

Her insight into the implications of
David's actions, her readiness to act and her humble
self-recriminations before David saved every male
member of the family. She had rightly discerned
that David intended to kill them because Nabal had
been dismissive of his regal dignity.

Abigail's beauty, charm, wit and wisdom impressed David, so that, when he heard that Nabal had died, David successfully proposed marriage to her. There is no record that she and Nabal had had children but she was David's second wife and bore him his second son (II Sam. 3:3).

Chapter 16

<u>Barren Women</u>

Childlessness was a condition which, until modern times, remained a reproach, even a disgrace to a married woman. For example, when, at last, Jacob's beloved wife, Rachel, bore a son she said:

"God has taken away my disgrace." (Gen. 30:23).

In similar circumstances Elizabeth, John the Baptist's mother, had comparable emotions, saying:

"The Lord has done this for me. In these days he has shown his favour and taken away my disgrace among the people." (Lk. 1:25)

When revealing to Elizabeth's kinswoman, Mary, the well kept secret of Elizabeth's pregnancy, the angel Gabriel announced:

"Even Elizabeth your relative is going to have a child in her old age, and she who was said to be barren is in her sixth month. For nothing is impossible with God." (Lk. 1:36-37)

In the matter of the heart's cry and prayer of the childless woman, Scripture many times bears out the truth of Gabriel's statement that nothing is impossible with God. Miraculous provision of babies for barren women is an important theme throughout Biblical history, and a distinct promise from the Lord:

"He settles the barren woman in her home as a happy mother of children." (Ps. 113:9)

Mary and Elizabeth would have had both a knowledge
and a real understanding of the story of Sarah, the
aged and barren matriarch of the Jewish people,
without whose son, Isaac, their people would not
have come into being. As women who were versed in
Judaism and the Hebrew Scriptures, the Tanach, they
would also have had a deep understanding of
Hannah's story, and the contribution that her 'little
miracle', Samuel, made to their people.

They would also have known that, although she was not
past the age of child-bearing, the matriarch Rachel's
pregnancies were only possible with Divine
intervention. This is clearly shown in the Tanach.
When the childless Rachel begged her husband,
Jacob, for children, the following exchange took
place: "Give me children, or I'll die" (Gen.
30:1b). Jacob then became angry with her and said,

> *"Am I in the place of God, who has kept you*
> *from having children?"* (Gen. 30:2)

Conversely any Hebrew woman who mothered many
children was considered to be blessed and fruitful,
honoured by her husband and others. Leah's pleasure
at bearing children was as much out of expectation of
earning her husband's love through it, as from the
desire to be a mother.

When Leah bore her first son she thought that her
husband would love her. By the time her third son was born
she would have been content for him to be attached to her.
Upon the birth of her sixth son she simply trusted that she

would deserve to be honoured by him, no longer regarding son-bearing as a tool to gain love.

Probably by this time relations between the two
sisters, Leah and Rachel, had not greatly improved.
Rachel was still childless and distressed, while Leah
had a daughter and six sons. Yet something had
happened to Leah in the intervening years.

While her concern had previously been to coax her husband's affections away from her sister, with the birth of her fourth son she redirected her orientation. She took her eyes off Jacob, and the thing she didn't have in her life, and looked to the Lord, saying: "This time I will praise the Lord." (Gen. 29:35).

The birth of Judah, whose name means `praise',
marked a real change of preoccupation and direction
in Leah's life. Her fifth son was named `Issachar'
after God's reward, and the name she chose for son
number six `Zebulun' (meaning `honour') indicates
acceptance of her standing in the family, and shows
that she no longer competed with Rachel, with
bitterness of heart.
And so it is that Leah, also, is honoured as a mother
in Israel. She praised God for her children, and she
praised Him despite the fact that things in the family
were not going her way, the needs of her ego were
not being met.
Leah came to love her children for
themselves, not for what they could buy for her from
her husband. When she gave birth to her sixth son
she made one of the greatest affirmations of

motherhood in all of Scripture: "*God has presented me with a precious gift.*" (Gen. 30:20)

Yet it is not the possessing of either husband or offspring which defines the status of `a mother in Israel', but the mother-like quality of the life; her relationship with God and her actions towards her fellows. Many of the greatest `mothers in Israel', like Naomi, Ruth, Anna and Judith were widows, while others, like Miriam, may never have married at all. In modern times, some, like Gladys Aylward, and Corrie Ten Boom, who remained unmarried, have been `mother' to spiritual children in many places.

> "`*Sing, O barren woman, you who never bore a child; burst into song, shout for joy, you who were never in labour; because more are the children of the desolate woman than of her who has a husband,' says the Lord.*" (Is. 54:1)

Chapter 17

<u>Three Unnamed Women of Faith</u>

1. A Prophet's Widow,

   2. A Woman of Shunem,

   3. A Woman of Zarepath

As in the case of Samson's mother, we have not been provided with the names of the Shunammite woman, nor the prophet's widow,

both of whose stories are recorded in II Kings, chapter four, nor with the name of the Zarepathite.

Each of these women emerge as 'mothers in Israel'.

Each achieved an increase in faith through obedience and trust in the word of the servants of the Lord, and saw miraculous results. In each story there is a clear indication of the powerful operation of the Holy Spirit

when women co-operate with the Lord, even in the simplest tasks of daily life.

Each woman's story began with a major lack, or cause of unhappiness. Each woman was dispirited, yet, in the very midst of her need, each obeyed the revelation she had been given, despite her mental reservations and emotional state. No elaborate ritual, nor

expensive sacrifice was required of the women; only simple acts of obedience. Like Deborah, each arose to respond.

<u>1) A Prophet's Widow</u>

This prophet's widow, aided by her sons, in simple obedience, borrowed jars from her neighbours and, in faith, despite the irrationality of the task, poured oil from her meagre supply into each

of them. What a simple, homely action: with what miraculous results !

Both of these women came through her encounter with the miraculous, with her faith in God strengthened. The Lord delights to

be the Father of orphans, Husband of widows and Provider for the needy. He rewarded each woman; alleviated her need-state and exchanged each garment of heaviness for a spirit of happiness.

<u>2) A Shunemite woman</u>

The life of a certain woman of Shunem, a village near Jezreel, in the area near Mt.Carmel, typifies many of the qualities of true mothers in Israel: she was hospitable, generous and caring. She was also

gifted with spiritual discernment and was spiritually receptive, though she could hardly be said to be full of faith. The woman, the wife of an older farmer of this fertile valley, obviously had a happy marital relationship as her husband readily agreed with all of her requests and her suggestions for assisting the prophet of God.

As a mother she was dedicated, devoted and loving to her son. In his illness she held onto hope while there was still life in her son, and she had faith in God, even when that life was gone. This mother in Israel kept her own counsel, and followed her own leading, single mindedly seeking the man of God, being turned aside from that path neither by her husband, nor the prophet's servant.

Although she chided Elisha for raising her hopes with the promise of a son, after the child died she knew whom to seek out and whom to

cling to, saying: "*As surely as the Lord lives and as you live, I will not leave you.*" (II Kng. 4:30)

When the prophet sensed the deep anguish of this mother's soul he immediately knew the answer to the question he had once asked:

"*You have gone to all this trouble for us.*
Now what can be done for you?"(II Kng. 4:13)

This Biblical narrative demonstrates the nature of a mother in Israel: hospitable, caring, loving and obedient to the word of the Lord. She

also returned deep gratitude to the Lord for the boy's life.

A final but most significant quality of this Shunammite woman was

her watchfulness. How many hours a mother hovers over the newborn baby, or the injured child, or holds the sick child as this mother did !

To keep watch in this way is also a characteristic of fathers; as well as mothers. God the Father is described as the watchman or guardian of Israel, the ʿshomerʾ, who never gives way to sleep:

"Indeed, he who watches over Israel will neither slumber nor sleep." (Ps. 121:3-4)

<u>C) A Woman of Zarepath</u>

In a similar vein, a certain poverty-stricken widow of the village of Zarephath, in South Lebanon, was in dire need. Her story is very much like that of the Shunammite woman, except that she gave hospitality to the prophet out of her dire poverty.

She too was obedient, faithful, and a loving mother. She, too, was rewarded for her service to the prophet of God. She, too, received her loved one back from death when son was raised from death by Elijah (I Kings 17). Each found that her spiritual discernment and

faith in the God of Israel grew. The woman of Zarepath was a gentile, and her saga demonstrates that non-Jews can indeed be `mothers in Israel'.

Centuries later Jesus praised her, and acknowledged her place, even as a gentile, in the chronicle of Israel:

*"I assure you that there were many widows in Israel in
Elijah's time, when the sky was shut for three and a half
years and there was a severe famine throughout the land. Yet
Elijah was not sent to any of them, but to a widow in Zarepath
in the region of Sidon."* (Lk. 4:25-26)

Each of these three unnamed women demonstrates the qualities which earn them our deep respect as `mothers in Israel': hospitality, dedication to their children, obedience, and faith in the God of Israel - coupled with action.

While asking "who is a mother in Israel?" we are reminded of the One who is `Abba'; our Father. Like the mother of Shunem, the `mother in Israel' keeps watch over Israel with love, especially when the land is in need, or its life hangs in the balance.

At times the threat to Israel's life may be well hidden, politically concealed, only spiritually discernable, as when Syrian troops had penetrated into the Galilee on Yom Kippur of 1973, hours before Israeli's had any inkling that their territory had been invaded. Such events remind us of the need for the watchmen and watchwomen over Israel:

"I have posted watchmen on your walls, O Jerusalem;
they will never be silent day or night." (Is. 62:6a)

Chapter 18

<u>Esther</u>

A whole book of the Hebrew Bible is devoted to the story of this orphaned Jewish refugee called Hadassah, who was raised by her older cousin, Mordecai, during the reign of Xerxes of Persia (486-465 B.C.E.). Not only that but the book commands Jews to remember and celebrate her deed: which they still do at Purim

every year.

Mordecai does not seem to have had employment because he walked in the courtyard of the harem or sat at the king's gate every day, hoping to find out how his ward (now called Esther) was faring.

He may have wanted to utilise Esther's beauty to secure her financial future.

Xerxes was a despot and his treatment of women was very autocratic, for example, he demoted his wife Vashti because she declined to obey him. A "bride show" of virgins was held to select a new queen (a custom that was adopted in the Christian Byzantine Empire hundreds of years later) and Esther was one of the girls chosen to undergo twelve months of beauty preparation before she could spend one night with the king. Women had no say in when they would lose their virginity, nor to whom (Est. 2:14).

Rulers had wives, concubines and many sex-slaves and Esther lived in Xerxes' harem with his concubines before being selected as queen (v. 12).

It was divine protection that guided this selection of Esther as queen rather than as a concubine. She received her elevated station in

order to save the Jewish people from murderous intent; just as Mordecai had saved the King Xerxes from an assassination plot (Est. 2:21-23).

When Mordecai refused to kneel down in homage to the official, Haman, hatred consumed Haman so that he determined to exterminate all Jews, not knowing that Queen Esther was also Jewish. As Mordecai told Esther, she was the only person who could

save them all from the king's edict of annihilation. Because she was reluctant, fearing the wrath of the king, Mordecai sent her this

message: "Do not think that because you are in the king's house you alone of all the Jews will escape. For if you remain silent at this time, relief and deliverance for the Jews will arise from another place, but you and your father's family will perish. And who knows but that you have come to royal position for such a time as this." (Est. 4:14)

Esther feared that she had fallen from the king's favour (4:11) and knew that to approach him unbidden was against the law so she asked that all of the Jews would fast from food and water for three

days as she and her maidens would. She accepted the possibility that it might cost her her life (4:16).

The outcome of the matter was that Haman was hanged on the gallows he had prepared for Mordecai, the Jews were saved and Mordecai was raised to be second only to the king in authority (10:3).

The text stresses Esther's obedience to Mordecai and her beauty.

She also had inner strength and intelligence and she did not harbour resentment against the males in the story. There is no record that she bore a child to the king but she was a mother in Israel because she chose to try to save the Jewish people even if she paid for it

with her own life.

Chapter 19

The Seventh Night of Hanukkah

On the seventh evening of the eight day celebration
of Hanukkah, which the New Testament calls the
Feast of the Dedication, women are remembered in a
special way. Hanukkah is a commemoration of a
miracle provided for Israel during times of great
national threat in the Inter-Testament period. The
narrative of this period is told in the two books of
Maccabees.
It is therefore fitting that the story of the
mother of the seven martyred sons, from the Book of
Maccabees, is read on this evening. A second story
which centres on a Jewish heroine is also recounted.
This is the story of Judith. While Judith resembles
Hulda, her story, in many respects, resembles that of
Deborah.

Women, who are the kindlers of both spiritual and
physical light in the home, are honoured at
Hanukkah, as they light the Hanukkoi flames. But this
honour is not exclusive to the seventh night, nor to
the eight day feast of Hunnakah. It enhances every
Sabbath table, when the mother lights the Sabbath

candles and the priest in the home, in honour of his wife,
reads from the Tanach, from the thirty-first
chapter of Proverbs.
The two stories read at Hanukkah are from Hebrew
tradition, commonly called the `Apocrypha' but they
are contain spiritual truth. The mother's story is
entirely in keeping with the state of oppression, and
suppression of Jewish national and religious identify,
which spurred the Jewish Revolt under the
Maccabees.
Circumcision and Sabbath observance were forbidden, the
Temple was desecrated with pig's
blood, Feasts of Bacchus were imposed, and pork-
eating was required of the Jews of Judea. (Enforced
eating of pig-flesh has always been a common
persecution of Jews.
For example the `maranos' in 14th Century Spain were
given their insulting title because it means `pig-eaters'. Proof of
their `true conversion' to Roman Catholicism was the eating of
pork).
This unnamed mother in Israel is not remembered
only for her courage under persecution and suffering,
but for her godly example and encouragement. She
encouraged each of her boys to fix their vision on
their Sovereign Lord.
Her example of righteous love
enabled each of the boys to pronounce righteous
judgement upon their tormentors, without hatred.
Not one of them recanted, not even the youngest,
whose demeanour so attracted the admiration of

Antiochus Epiphanes, his tormentor, that he personally pleaded with him, with attractive promises,

to come over to the opposition.

Their final testimony was a sanctification of the Name of God:

> *"The king of the world shall raise up us, who*
> *have died for his laws, unto an eternal renewal*
> *of life."* (II Maccabees 7:9)

This gallant mother, whose grave, tradition holds, is near the blue domed tomb in Safed, gave more to her sons in one day than she had given all their lives. Of her it is written:

> *"But above all was the mother marvellous and*
> *worthy of honourable memory; for when she*
> *looked on seven sons perishing within the*
> *space of one day, she bare the sight with a*
> *good courage for the hopes that she had set on*
> *the Lord."* (II Mac. 7:20)

This mother's story of heroism and courage reminds me of Gladys Aylward. This diminutive chong-sam clad woman was already a living legend when she recounted, in my presence, the ordeal of having to watch the communist Chinese kill her adopted sons and daughters.

These were the very same children she had previously rescued from the invading Japanese army. As young adults they were each shot for refusing to renounce their Christian faith.

The Small Woman, a British citizen, and her younger children, were forced to watch their martyrdom.

On one day Gladys Aylward lost many children. They
received the martyr's crown, and, like Gladys, the
pious and righteous mother in Israel lost many sons
in one day. Their sufferings were extreme, but their
testimonies were undiminished. The Scriptural
account then records their mother's death:
"And last of all after her sons the mother died."
(ll Mac. 7:41)
We assume that this heroine mother was killed by
those who murdered her seven sons so cruelly, but
she may have died of grief or shock, having held
herself together just long enough to support and
encourage her sons, before herself succumbing.
Perhaps she was like the matriarch Sarah, whose
death is recorded in Genesis just after the story of the
akedah (the testing of Abraham).

Surely the akedah was also a supreme test of Sarah's mother-heart. The great Rabbi Rashi suggested that Sarah died of shock upon hearing that Isaac had been taken to be sacrificed.

Another view holds that she died in profound ecstasy; her most significant mission
accomplished. She knew that Isaac was returned to
her alive, having been willing to obey God unto
death.
During the Feast of Hanukkah, a second woman,
Judith, is also honoured. Judith's contribution to the
welfare of Israel was in the spirit of Miriam, Deborah,

Ruth and Jael. Like Deborah she was an encourager; and an exhorter, even of the men in the civil and military leadership. Like Hulda she was a prophetess to whom the city leaders came for counsel, saying:

> *All that thou hast spoken hast thou spoken*
> *with a good heart, and there is none that shall*
> *gainsay thy words. For this is not the first day*
> *wherein thy wisdom is manifested; but from*
> *the beginning of thy days all people have*
> *known thy under-standing, because the*
> *disposition of thy heart is good."*

(Judith 8:28-9)

Like Deborah, Judith was a woman of action, and like Ruth, and the later prophetess, Anna, she was a virtuous and godly widow, given to prayer and fasting. Like Jael, she single handedly killed an enemy leader, having tempted him to his death with her wiles. In the footsteps of Miriam she led the people of Israel in joyful dance of thanksgiving and like both Deborah and Miriam she composed songs of praise: *Begin unto my God with timbrels, Sing unto my Lord with cymbals; Tune unto him psalm and praise; Exalt him and call upon his name."* (Judith 16:2)

Chapter 20

<u>Elizabeth</u>

When Elizabeth (in Hebrew, Elisheva) held her only child in her arms she knew that she was holding a miracle, a promised miracle that she and Zechariah (Z'kharyah) had held fast to since before the boy was conceived. She knew that, being old, she may not live to see her son fulfil his destiny, perhaps she would not live to see his Bar Mitzvah, but she determined to do every thing in her power to set his feet upon the right path. This was the path which Gabriel had explained to Zechariah in the Holy Place of the Temple in Jerusalem, (Lk.1:8-22).

Her son would touch no unclean thing, he would drink no wine, only pure water - water from the desert springs in the wilderness. He would be dedicated to the Lord - a Nazarite from birth. Johanan (John) was not to be one, like Paul, who made the customary temporary Nazarite vow, (Acts. 21:26). He was to be a perpetual Nazarite, totally set apart, dedicated to the Lord - korban.

Sometimes Elizabeth would have remembered Samson, the Nazarite from days of old, who had also been born to a barren woman by Divine intervention. No doubt, at such times, Elizabeth prayed fervently the her son would not desecrate his Nazarite vows as Samson had done many times. She would have prayed that her son be strong enough to avoid the temptations of pagan women.

Like Samson's parents, Elizabeth and Zechariah were resolved that their son's upbringing would be God-ordained.

Perhaps Elizabeth also meditated on the similarities of the angelic visitations with which each father-to-be was given the good news. Perhaps she thought about the awe of The Majesty experienced by Manoah and his wife as they fell on their faces on the ground, when their sacrifice was accepted by Him.

Obviously Gabriel's appearance meant that the sacrifice of incense, which her own husband had offered in the Temple at a similar moment, was also accepted.

Her son, her little miracle, would no doubt look like a wild man in the desert, with unshaven face and uncut hair, but he followed in noble footsteps: not Samson's, but Elijah's. He was to be one like Elijah. His was an Elijah task; and Elizabeth knew that he was to prepare the way for Messiah: that One whose identity she was privileged to know, even before Mary had given birth to Him.

John was to be the voice crying in the wilderness, just as Elijah cried out against the apostasy of Israel. If her son's ministry was to be in the desert then he must grow up there; not in the unruly city, nor the Hellenised temple court circles and luxurious palaces, and certainly not amidst the sophisticated corruption of Herod's Jerusalem.

John, as the son of a cohen, a priest of the Lord, with a prophetic calling and righteous upbringing, was more than eligible to aspire to the high priesthood. Elizabeth knew, however, that little Yohanan (John) must not grow up amid the moral and spiritual decay of a Temple system controlled by the pagan Romans, under a Roman appointed High Priest. And so it was that Yohanan was in the desert `until': until the word of God came to him. From this time on he knew that his life's work (however short) had begun.

John may have lived for a time with the Essenes, or some other Qumran community. Almost certainly he knew of them and trod the same dusty tracks through the wilderness. Those stony hills were a wasteland - once the haunt of brigands and wild animals, made famous by the parable of the man who went down from Jerusalem to Jericho, where he fell among thieves. To this day the Wilderness of Judea remains the inhospitable home of the tent dwelling Bedouin, with their little flocks of sheep and goats.

The Essenes had their own theology, their own vision of the future; whereas John had God-revealed theology and his own unique and independent destiny to fulfil. Therefore John was found, at about thirty years of age, near the Jordan River: "*Preaching a baptism of repentance for the forgiveness of sins.*" (Lk. 3:3)

From the time of his birth, John, like Samuel before him, was given by his righteous and devout parents `unto Israel'; and unto the Lord, Who had first given him to them. John came to fulfil the prophesy that `Elijah must come first' and to do a work of preparation for the soon-coming Messiah.

This work was in accordance with the vision revealed to his father, Zechariah, in the Holy Place, while he was burning incense on Israel's behalf:

> *"And you, my child, will be called a prophet of the Most High; for you will go on before the Lord to prepare the way for him, to give his people the knowledge of salvation through the forgiveness of their sins, because of the tender mercy of our God."* (Lk. 1:76-78b)

It is fitting that the angel Gabriel appeared to the priest Zechariah as he burned incense on the altar of incense within the Temple, because this daily ritual represented the offering up of the prayers of all the people. The honour of exercising this priestly duty was decided by the drawing of lots, and a priest could wait all his life for just one such privilege.

The timing was exactly right. Zechariah's turn came about sixteen months before the Messiah was due to be born, that is, in the fullness of God's time. This exact timing gave Elizabeth the five months of seclusion she needed (while her pregnancy was kept from becoming public knowledge), before Mary visited her, bearing her own amazing news. Although Zechariah's lifetime opportunity came very late in his years of faithful priestly ministry, it came exactly on time.

Mother-in-Israel do not give up. God's time is exactly right. Will you release your child for a unique and God-given work of preparation for the soon-coming

Messiah of Israel? Your child can be a prophetic voice to this generation; as Elijah was to his. Like the forerunner, Yohanan, he, or she, is eligible to become a priest of the Lord:

> "(Jesus) *has freed us from our sins by his blood, and has made us to be a kingdom of priests to serve his God and Father - to him be glory and power forever and ever! Amen.*"
>
> (Rev. 1:6)

Chapter 21

<u>Mary</u>

When the Lord had need of a man to be His
emissary on earth the prophet Isaiah made a deep
pledge of obedience to his God, a response of heart
commitment and dutiful servant-hood. Isaiah followed
the example of the patriach Abraham who stood,
knife in hand, before the altar of sacrifice. Isaiah used
the same Hebrew expression of submission found in
Genesis 22:11 - Hineni (Here I am).
Isaiah's `hineni' commitment involved both
action and conviction: faith and works. "Here am I,
send me." (Is. 6:8)
Similarly Mary was asked to make a profound
commitment which would require of her the deepest
faith, the most ernest commitment and the most
demanding action. A mother was needed, a woman
with a true servant spirit, resolute courage, physical
stamina, dignity and deep spirituality.
The request of the angel, Gabriel, messenger
of the Most High, was Mary's own `hineni' challenge.
Her response expressed first submissive and obedient
servant-hood; and secondly faith in God's plan for her
life:
*"Behold the handmaiden of the Lord, be it unto
me according to thy word"* (Luke 1:38 A.V.)
Mary's womanhood, her maidenhood, her body, her
reputation, perhaps her betrothal to the good man

Joseph, probably her standing within family and community, maybe even life itself, was weighed for a moment on the balance of time.

While Mary's natural reasoning failed to comprehend, her soul responded willingly, her faith triumphed. Her heart said `hineni' -

I am here, I am willing, I will see this task through, whatever the cost.

We must be forever grateful for that response. While, in a split second of time, Eve had chosen to doubt the word of God, Mary, at a similar moment of challenge, chose to submit, to obey and to trust her Lord.

The seed of the woman, Mary, would be born to crush the head of the serpent, and so nullify the mistake of

Eve, the woman who was wounded, who `fell'.

The fear of affording Jesus' mother undue homage has robbed Mary of the honour which her contribution to our faith deserves: a contribution that was essential to Eternal deliverance.

What Miriam accomplished for the endangered infant Moses, and for the Jewish people, in distant Egypt, Mary accomplished, for the endangered infant Jesus, and for all mankind, when she made a perilous escape

across the Sinai Desert into Egypt, and back.

Mary's surrendered her own plans and desires, and her own physical body, to become the `Christ bearer'.

The submission of her heart to the piercing of the soul, as mother of the Crucified One, speaks to every woman who must accept an unfulfilled plan, a shattered dream, a forlorn hope.

It speaks to every mother who must face the difficult choice to carry in her body the unplanned, the extra-marital, the rejected, the deformed. It speaks to every human being, in every age, who must endure despair, death, or a broken heart.

Although Mary did not know of these immortal words they were richly true of her life: "*That Christ may be formed in you.*" (Gal. 4:19)

The life of this young mother was motherhood in extremis: in labour on a donkey's back, in childbirth in a crude stable; in life-threatening danger as a fugitive in the desert; a refugee, an alien in a heathen land. Yet she was the ʻChrist keeper', His most faithful nurturer, ally, disciple and friend. In the secret fastness of her heart Mary's commitment was for life: and beyond. It is fitting that, between the Passover crucifixion and the Day of Pentecost, all the disciples continually gatherd for prayer in an upper room, with Mary, a unique ʻmother in Israel':

"*They all joined together constantly in prayer, along with the women and Mary, the mother of Jesus, and his brothers.*" (Act.1:14)

Mary and Elizabeth

Luke allows us to catch a glimpse of a unique relationship in Mary's early life, a shared sisterhood that went beyond the ordinary affinity which two pregnant women often share. It is not surprising that Mary hastened to visit Elizabeth when the angel Gabriel revealed that the older woman was six

months into a miraculous but well concealed
pregnancy.
Mary and Elizabeth were bound together
by ties of blood-relationship and, despite the age
difference, by friendship. Mary was obviously
prepared to trust Elizabeth with her secret.
From the moment Mary entered the home of her
kinswoman they were bound together by wonder,
and the thrill of their unique experiences, and later by
shared confidences as they told their respective
stories.

Both women instantly and simultaneously received
prophetic insights into the Divine mystery in
which they were participants. Mary and Elizabeth
knew what no other women knew, and were
endowed with a God-given anointing as no others.
We can visualise them living together for three
months, as their sons grew within them, singing songs of
praise as they joyfully prepared infant garments and baked
bread in the little home amongst
the hills
. Was the home in the village of Ein Karem, and did Mary
draw water from the ancient spring known to this day as Spring
of the Virgin? Only oral tradition says that it was so.
Wherever their home, and despite her husband's
temporary muteness, Elizabeth's encouragement, the
wisdom of her years, and her prophetic anointing
would have been of great support to Mary as she
faced the necessity of returning to her community
and all that her future would entail.

We do not know that Mary ever visited the home of Elizabeth and Zechariah with the infant Jesus. She certainly was unable to until her return from Egypt; but the affinity between these mothers was probably significant in forging the bond that existed between their sons, who were born so close in time, so entwined in eternal destiny.

If deliverance for Israel, what-ever the cost, is a central attribute in the life of a ʽmother in Israel' then these two Jewish women, Elizabeth and her youthful friend and kinswoman Mary, are most worthy of the title.

Chapter 22

<u>The Other Maries:</u>

1) Women played an often overlooked but very significant role in Jesus' ministry, and in its climax - the Easter story. It was women who were Jesus' most faithful companions during his last hours of suffering on earth. Women accompanied him along his terrible via dolorosa:

> *"A large number of people followed him, including women who mourned and wailed for him."*(Lk. 23.27)

2) Many women kept their long vigil beside his cross:

"Many women were there, watching from a distance. They had followed him from Galilee

to care for his needs." (Mt. 27:55)

3) While Nicodemus wrapped his body in cloths with seventy-five pounds of myrrh and aloes, and Joseph of Arimathea laid the Master to rest in his own new tomb, women continued their vigil by his grave:

> *"Mary Magdalene and the other Mary were sitting there across from the tomb."* (Mat. 27:61)

Women accompanied his body from the scene of his death to the tomb, and then returned home to properly prepare for his burial rites:

> *"The women who had come with Jesus from Galilee followed Joseph and saw the tomb and how his body was laid in it. Then they went home and prepared spices and perfumes."*

(Luk. 23:55)

Women were the first to visit his grave and to discover his empty tomb. While the apostles were rebuked for their stubborn refusal to believe the eyewitness accounts (Mk.16:14), the women were the first to hear the angel's message and to believe that he was indeed risen:

> *"When they came back from the tomb, they*
> *told all these things to the Eleven, and to all*
> *the others. It was Mary Magdalene, Joanna,*
> *Mary the mother of James, and the others*
> *with them who told this to the apostles. But*
> *they did not believe the women, because their*
> *words seemed to them like nonsense."* (Lk. 24:9-11)

How often have women's words of wisdom seemed like nonsense?

One of these devoted women, the beloved Mary Magdalene, as well as being one of the first witnesses to his resurrection, was the one to whom Jesus first spoke words of comfort and reassurance (Jn. 20:10-18).

The myrrh-bearers who went to the tomb to embalm the body were not exactly the same women, nor the same number of women who had stood by Jesus' cross. Perhaps their individual contributions are overlooked because many of them bore the same name: Mary. Mary was such a well-used name that it was over-used. The Hebrew name was actually

Miriam, a most popular name in the period because of the influence of the Jewish heroine, Miriam the prophetess, Moses' sister.

The Gospel of Mark records the presence, both at the cross and at the tomb on the morning of the resurrection, of three women.

(1) Mary of Magdala,

(2) Mary the Mother of James the younger and Joseph,

(3) and Salome (see Mk. 15:40; 16:1; Mat. 27:56).

Matthew's Gospel (Chapter 27) agrees with 1 and 2 (above) but calls the third woman "the mother of the sons of Zebedee". Now the sons of Zebedee were the principal disciples, James and John, so one of the women at the tomb was the wife of the Galilean fisherman, Zebedee. It generally accepted that her name was Salome. She was the third woman at the tomb named by Mark.

Luke agrees with the other chroniclers that Mary Magdalene went early to the tomb, stating that she was accompanied by women he referred to as "Mary the Mother of James; Joanna and others" (Lk. 24:10).

While there is certainly full agreement as to Mary Magdalene's presence, can we completely reconcile the four gospel records? Salome, the wife of Zebedee had a son called James (actually Jacob) and scholars sometimes refer to her as Mary Salome.

John's Gospel clearly states that Mary, Jesus' mother,

was present at the cross.

"Near the cross of Jesus
stood his mother, his mother's sister, Mary the
wife of Clopas, and Mary Magdalene." (Jn. 19:23)
John and the Synoptic gospels agree that both Mary
Magdelene and Jesus' mother, Mary, were near him
at his cross. The oracle of the prophet Simeon came
to pass:

"This child is destined to cause the falling and
rising of many in Israel, and to be a sign that
will be spoken against, so that the thoughts of
many hearts will be revealed. And a sword will
pierce your own soul too." (Lk. 2:34-35)

Turn momentarily to the other women in the story,
Joanna. She is mentioned twice in Luke's narrative;
first as one of the group of women who provided
financial support of Jesus and secondly as being one
of the group of grieving women who went to the
tomb.

She is probably the sometimes unnamed
woman in the group, unnamed, perhaps, because she
was the least notable although she was well
connected, as the wife of Chuza, Herod Antipas's
steward, and she contributed finances to the group
(Lk. 8:1-3 and 24:1-10).

Although Luke indicates there were other, unnamed
women in the group of female supporters, as quoted
above, John's Gospel suggests the presence of four
women at the cross: Jesus' mother, her sister, Mary
Magdalene, and yet another Mary - the wife of

Clopas.
Clopas is believed by scholars to have been
either Joseph's brother or Mary's brother and almost
certainly the disciple Cleopas, who met Jesus near
Emmaus [Luk. 24:18]. Of these, only the identity of
Jesus' aunt, his mother's sister, is concealed by this
writer, although not by Mark.
Just as the gospel writer, St John, avoided calling
himself by name, but used the appellation "the
disciple whom Jesus loved" so his own mothers' name
may have been concealed. Mary's sister was probably
Salome, whom Mark referred to as the third woman
present.

The obvious devotion between Jesus and his disciple
John, plus John's presence with the women at the
cross, and the select status of both of Zebedee's
sons, fits the scenario that they were all immediate
family members.
How fitting that from his cross Jesus
entrusted his mother into the care of his most
beloved disciple, his cousin John, who, alone of all the
disciples, stood near the cross comforting his mother
and aunt, and whose entire family was so supportive
of his ministry from the earliest days in Galilee (see Jn.
19:26-27).
Remember that James' and John's mother made a
request - that they, Zebedee's sons, would occupy
chief places of honour in the Kingdom? Just the sort

of favour an aunty would expect for her boys! This would mean that both Mary and her sister, Salome, had sons named James - James Bar-Zebedee was the older.

Hence Mary was the mother of 'James the younger' (as Mark 15:40 says). In such a close family

it would have been very important to find some way to distinguish between the two cousins but most unlikely that Jesus' mother, the Virgin Mary, would have been identified only by another son's name. Many scholars, however, accept that Mary Clopas was the mother of James and Joseph/Joses.

Towards the end of Jesus' ministry there was an outer circle of women supporters and contributors, who provided hospitality and finances; and a smaller, inner group of women, blood relatives and very close friends who became the chief-mourners. This group seems to have included five women: Mary; her sister Salome; Mary Magdelene; Joanna, and Mary Clopas, whose husband Clopas, was a disciple and probably a relative.

A sixth woman, Susanna, is named in Luke 10:3 as a financial contributor, but nothing else is

known about her.

What role did the myrrh-bearing women fulfil? Nicodemus brought seventy-five pounds of myrrh and aloes, a large quantity that had to be mixed and prepared as soon as the Sabbath was over, so the women worked all night, only to find the tomb empty, except for one or two angel messengers.

The roles which these staunch and faithful servants played in the gospel story have many examples and lessons to teach us: lessons of fidelity, endurance, devotion and self-sacrifice.

Many of those lessons are embodied in the actions of yet another Mary: Mary of Bethany. This was the Mary who meekly and humbly sat at Jesus' feet, gazing up into his face, to absorb his teachings and his words of wisdom, her eyes and her ears fixed intently upon him.

This was the woman of whom Jesus said: "*Mary has chosen the betuer part*".

She was also the one who anointed him for his burial with her most costly possession? She was the one who lay her life at his feet, with tears ... the one who bathed his feet with her tears and dried them with her long flowing hair? (Jn. 11:2).

There is another account of a similar anointing, in Galilee rather than in Bethany, and much earlier in Jesus' ministry (Lk. 7:37-50) where the woman is described as a sinner.

Both demonstrate the devotion of women to the Lord and were prophetic acts. Jesus, himself, interpreted the later anointing as a preparation for his burial (Jn. 12:7) it happened only six days before the Passover on which he would die and the day before the first Palm Sunday (12:1, 13).

Chapter 23

<u>Secrets of the Virtuous Wife</u>

The Jewish ideal woman comes in three varieties:

- EshahHakhamah
- EshaHashuvah and
- EshahGdolah

The first of these is the wise woman who is intelligent and alert, possessed of innate intelligence,
learning and an inquiring mind. The second is the dignified woman, characterised by inner pride and dignity. She has an honourable spirit, living above gossip, the petty and the vulgar,
however, is the great woman.

She combines two characteristics that appear to be mutually exclusive: unshakable determination and humility. She is simultaneously both shy and iron willed, both meek and fearless, quiet and forthright, a devoted follower and an indomitable leader. The biblical heroines are of this ilk: "Strength and dignity are her clothing" (Prov. 31:25).

According to Scripture the good wife is a woman of charity towards the needy, *"She opens her arms to the poor and extends her hands to the needy"* (Prov. 31: 20). She diligently cares for her family with her cooking and gets them safely

through the snows of winter with home-made
quilts and warm garments (31:15, 21-22).
The good wife is not cloistered at home nor restricted
in rights but goes out and about in pursuit of her
business interests, ensuring that they are profitable.
She creates goods, which are on-sold by the
merchant class. She is skilled in textile production and
is both a businesswoman and a land-owner.

> *"She considers a field and buys it, out of her*
> *earnings she plants a vineyard... she see that*
> *her trading is profitable. She makes linen*
> *garments and sells them, and supplies the*
> *merchants with sashes."* (Prov. 31:16, 18a, 24)

But, contrary to popular opinion, it is neither her
housekeeping skills nor her commercial exploits for
which the Virtuous Wife of Proverbs 31 is most
blessed; although these were indeed exemplary.
It is for the deliverance which her works secure for her
family; deliverance from need, fear, cold and want;
and for her spirituality: her faithful instruction,
wisdom, and fear of the Lord.

> "She speaks with wisdom, and faithful
> instruction is on her tongue.... Charm is
> deceptive and beauty is fleeting; but a woman
> who fears the Lord is to be praised." (Prov. 31:26, 30)

The Virtuous Wife embodies those qualities which the
God of Israel looks for in all of His people: dedication,
sweet smelling fragrance, fruitfulness, spirituality and
acts of charity; qualities of which He, Himself, is the
only source; qualities which are equally available to

women and to men:
> *"I will pour out my Spirit on all people.. your
> sons and your daughters.... Even on my
> servants; both men and women, I will pour out
> my Spirit in those days."* (Joel 2:28-29)

THE VINEYARD PARABLE

"

This is why Israel was chosen; for which we are
chosen: to bear fruit, to delight the Lord; to produce
`wine`, the Biblical symbol of joy. This is why the
Virtuous Wife from the book of Proverbs is so
admired as the ideal of Jewish married womanhood.
This is why, in the Jewish family, at every Shabbat
table, this passage from Proverbs is read by the
husband as a tribute to honour his wife.

Chapter 24

<u>Four Heroines in the Holocaust</u>
<u>Roza Robota, Ala Gertner, Regina Safirsztajn,</u>
<u>Ester (Estusia) Wajcblum.</u>

The story of these four young martyrs of Auschwitz-Birkenau is remarkable. Rosa, Ala, Regina and Ester were all hanged by the Nazis on 5th January, 1945. They had endured weeks of torture and interrogation aimed at forcing them to betray their co-conspirators in the partially successful plot to slow the rate of extermination by sabotage of the crematoria.

Rosa, Ala, Regina and Ester were all slave labourers in the Auschwitz III Unionwerke munitions factory. For eight months they smuggled tiny amounts of gunpowder concealed in the seams of their clothing, to the Jewish Under-ground, which actually succeeded in using the explosives. Five hundred of the Jewish prisoners who removed the dead from the gas-chambers perished in the slave-labourers revolt, which accompanied the explosion and the fire it triggered off in Crematorium III.

Professor Israel Gutman, then a 21 year old member of the underground in Auschwitz, attributes his own survival, and that of thirty others, to the heroic endurance of these four young women, under torture. Under Rosa Robota's leadership they were willing volunteers. They placed the needs of their people, who were being slaughtered in their thousands every day, above their own relative (but perhaps momentary) security.

The Memorial Sculpture at Yad Vashem in Jerusalem features these four heroines of Auschwitz: Roza Robota, Ala Gertner, Regina Safirsztajn and Ester (Estusia) Wajcblum who were martyred by the Nazis on 5/1/'45.

These four truly ` mothers in Israel': women of action, courage and determination, whose commitment said "whatever is needed, for as long as it takes". They did not die in vain: their deeds, in cooperation with the men they had assisted, saved some. They did not live to a marry, or to bear children, but they are of blessed memory. Every Jewish child born to those they saved, is their spiritual child. It may surely be said of them:

> "Sing, O barren woman, you who never bore a child, burst into song, shout for joy; you who were never in labour; because more are the children of the desolate woman than of her who has a husband."

> (Is. 54:1).

Plate 24.1. Memorial to four heroines of Auschwitz, at Yad Vashem. Photo: D. Campbell, 1990.

Chapter 25

<u>Hannah Senesh</u>

Hannah Senesh - young, single, heroine, martyr - is
also a mother in Israel. While still in her teens she
made aliyah, alone, to the Land that the British called
Palestine. Hannah joined the British army,
volunteering, at the age of 23, to parachute behind
enemy lines in order to help the Resistance in
Yugoslavia, and, if possible, help to rescue the Jews
of her native Hungary, whose mass-extermination
was in full swing. After working with Tito's partisans
she crossed the border into Hungary. She was
arrested, imprisoned, tortured, murdered. In their
attempt to extract information the Nazis arrested her
mother and tried to use the threat to her own mother's life,
as the two women were imprisoned in
adjoining cells.

During five months of interrogation and torture Hannah
adhered to her own principles, staunchly and honourably
defiant to the end. Hannah epitomises noble womanhood.
Through her poem, Blessed is the match, which she entrusted to
fellow Zionist Reuven Dafni before her arrest, Hannah has left
a short but profound and moving statement of principles, her
testimony for posterity, her autobiography. It is such a unique
blend of feminine gentleness and unflinching courage!

MOTHERS IN ISRAEL

BLESSED IS THE MATCH

Blessed is the match

that is consumed

> *Blessed is the match*

> *that is consumed*

> *in kindling flame.*

> *in kindling flame.*

> *Blessed is the flame that burns*

> *in the secret fastness*

> *of the heart.*

> *Blessed is the heart*

> *with its strength to stop*

> *its beating for honour's sake.*

Hannah Senesch
  martyred for Israel 7/11/1944

Deborah, Judge of Israel, would have been proud
  that Hannah Senech, warrior for Israel, marched in
  her own footsteps.

Chapter 26

Golda Meir

Turning to the more recent annals of Israel's saga the contribution of former Prime Minister, Golda Meir, as a true `mother in Israel' comes to mind. Golda began life in Kiev, Ukraine, in 1898, as Goldie Mabovitch before moving to Wisconsin, U.S.A., in 1906. In America she adopted Zionist ideology and became politically involved. When she married Morris Myerson she became Goldie Myerson and, in 1921, the young couple made aliyah to Israel to become kibutzniks. This was the period of the British mandate over Palestine and Goldie was deeply involved in the Labour Movement and the women's labour movement in particular. She became a powerful spokesperson for the Zionist cause in negotiations with British authorities.

In 1946, Goldie became head of the Political Department of the Jewish Agency where she worked hard for the release of detainees and the many war-refugees who had violated Britain's harsh immigration regulations by arriving in Palestine without their consent. [Later, when she became Minister for Labour (from 1949 to 1956) she championed free immigration rights for Jews.] In May, 1948, Goldie was a signatory to Israel's Declaration of Independence and was elected to parliament the following year. She served in the

Knesset from 1949 to 1974 as Minister of Labour
(1949-1956), Foreign Minister (1956-1966) and
Prime Minister (1969-1974) in a coalition
government that emerged from the 6-Day War of June
1967.

In 1956, as was customary, their family name was
made more Hebraic and Goldie Myerson became
Golda Meir.

Golda Meir sought peace in the Middle East and also
made secret trips to the Jordanian border to meet
with King Abdullah I of Jordan, to try to establish
harmonious relations with Jordan. Unfortunately
Jordan committed troops in the Yom Kippur War of
1973, in conjunction the main protagonists, Egypt
and Syria, with the help of units from Morocco, Iraq
and Saudi Arabia and weapons and armaments from
the Soviet Union.

Golda Meir also engaged with African and non-
aligned countries, met with Pope Paul VI, and
improved relations with Germany. Golda Meir was a
memorable Israeli politician who helped found the
State of Israel in 1948 and served as its fourth
prime minister, being the first woman to do so and
one of the few women to be prime minister of any
country in the 20th Century. Golda lost her only son
in the defence of Israel, when she could have used
her position to keep him safe from frontline action.
Golda Meir was a courageous woman of action,
unflinching, yet compassionate and soft-hearted.
Every Israeli knows the story of how she bridged

every gap of age and status, and united herself with the joyful but weeping young soldiers at the Western Wall on that momentous day in 1967, when the Old City, with all its timeless significance, came, once, under Israel's sovereignty.

Plate 24.1. Prime Minister Golda Meir.
Public domain.

Chapter 27

<u>Who is a mother in Israel?</u>

If we accept that Father God loves Israel as His own dear child then it is obvious that His parental example should be emulated, and that specific Biblical teaching and precedent relating to love for Israel, should be followed.

Strange as it may seem, God's love is the love of a father and like that of a mother. Of Israel He said:

"As a mother comforts her child, so I will comfort you; and you will be comforted...."
(Is. 66:13)

(1) Like the Lord Himself, a `mother in Israel' is one who looks upon Israel as their child. A mother is a mother forever, therefore her child is her child forever. Even though such a mother may forget her child, the Lord, in complete and eternal commitment,
says of Israel:

"Can a mother forget the baby at her breast and have no compassion on the child she has borne? Though she may forget, I will not forget you !" (Is. 49:15)

(2) Secondly, that loving relationship must be

expressed in practical ways such as care, nurture,

feeding, comfort and self-sacrificing and risk-taking

love: "*Comfort, comfort my people, says your*

God. Speak tenderly to Jerusalem." (Is. 40:1)

The mother heart cannot stand passively by. *What mother treats her child this way?*

(3) Softness, gentle handling and compassion, even for the unlovely, the deformed, the physically repulsive, are universally accepted characteristics of motherhood.
In this we directly follow Our Father's own example:
> "*On the day you (Jerusalem) were born your*
> *cord was not cut, nor were you washed with*
> *water to make you clean, nor were you rubbed*
> *with salt, or wrapped in cloths. No one looked*
> *on you with pity or had compassion enough to*
> *do these things for you..... Then I passed by*
> *and saw you kicking about in your blood, and*
> *as you lay there in your blood I said to you*
> "*Live!*"*.... I bathed you in water and washed*
> *the blood from you and put ointments on*
> *you...*"(Ez. 16:16)

Even when Israel failed to appreciate the care
bestowed upon her, she was not rejected, as this

story of Jerusalem's birth goes on to explain:
*"I will remember the covenant I made with
you in the days of your youth, and I will
establish an everlasting covenant with you.
Then you will remember your ways and be
ashamed... and you will know that I am the
Lord. Then I will make atonement for all you
have done..."* (Ez. 16:60-63)

(4) An active, assertive, `mother lioness' stance is
also needed, in the spirit of Deborah, who gave
leadership. This must be God-inspired assertiveness,
a prophetic voice, not pride and dominance.
These require a unique and delicate balance, a
Biblical blend of both strength and gentle
compassion: neither spineless nor heartless, but
openly demonstrating both backbone and heart. St
Paul's lifetime of enduring hardship demonstrated
such a combination, in fact in Galatians 4:19, in his
earnest desire to see his spiritual children created he
pictured himself, metaphorically, as a mother in pains
of childbirth and to the Thessalonians he wrote: *"We
were gentle among you like a mother caring
for her little children."* (I Thes. 2:7)

(5) The Lord's prophetic pronouncements and words
of encouragement and counsel will come forth as the
mother-in-Israel is active and takes courage.

(6) Worship and joyful praise, with dancing and music, will characterise the leadership of a mother in Israel. It is a woman's task to arouse, or at least to encourage the people in this aspect of congregational and personal life, as Miriam did.

(7) Finally, the evidence of true motherhood in Israel will be that deliverance is accomplished: a degree of physical, emotional or spiritual salvation. This may include deliverance from poverty, hunger, cold, sorrow, ignorance, fear, bitterness, spiritual malaise, suffering, lack of faith, persecution, or anti-Semitism; in short - a bringing of salvation to the earth, a bringing of light to a group or to a nation.

The prophet Isaiah spoke of Israel's failure to be truly the people of God, their failure to be fruitful as true mothers:

> *"We were with child, we writhed in pain, but we gave birth to wind. We have not brought salvation to the earth, we have not given birth to people of the world."* (Is. 26:18)

In contrast, those women who are most honoured in the records of the Tanach were noted for the deliverance and salvation which their decisive actions procured for Israel. Time and again women were the instruments of deliverance: Deborah, Jael, Zipporah, Esther, Rahab, Abigail, Judith, and many more. These women were not just noted for their practical action, but also for their personal spirituality and their outstanding spiritual leadership. Queen Esther, through self-sacrifice, prayer, fasting and spiritual leadership saved the entire people from threatened genocide. Deliverance for the Jews arose when Esther acted, just as Mordechi indicated it would. (Est. 4:8, 14)

*****

Mother-in-Israel, are you holding on to this promise?
*"All your sons will be taught by the Lord, and
great will be your children's peace."*

(Is. 54:13)

Holding onto such promises of Scripture, in faith, is
one of the greatest things you can do on behalf of
your child, the second is to set an example of what
you want your child to do and to be, so that you can
honestly and unashamedly say "be immitators of me".

******

Also by Deslee Campbell

The Topkapi Beggar
Voices From The Silence
Why a Roman Emperor Rebuilt Jerusalem and Jerash
Stones, Walls and Watchmen
Mothers in Israel
Ecclesia a Long Journey to Tomorrow

Watch for more at www.synagogueandchurch.com.

About the Author

Deslee Campbell, a former teacher of modern history, who worked in the field of educational psychology andcounselling.She has a Bachelor of Arts degree from the University of New South Wales, a Diploma in Education from the University of Sydney, and a Graduate Diploma in School Counselling from U.W.S/Nepean.She was has a Masters degree fromMacquarie University in early Christian Studies and a Phd from Sydney University.Deslee has visited Israel nine times, the first being in January 1970. During Passover 1990 Deslee was one of threeAustralians to visit the U.S.S.R. Since 1988 Deslee, and her late husband John, .they lived with their three sons and their adopted daughter in Sydney and attend a local Anglican Church in Sydney, Now widowed, Deslee has four children and three grandchildren.Her published works include the sequel novel, Love is a Journey, which follows Karen Evan's career as a nurse.With her son, Rev. Justin Campbell, she has co-authored a major 2-volume work in the mini-series Synagogue andChurch and her YouTube presentations can be viewed via the web addresshttp://www.synagogueandchurch.com

Read more at www.synagogueandchurch.com.